MUSIC ON THE
SHAKESPEARIAN STAGE

AMS PRESS
NEW YORK

An Elizabethan consort playing music for a masque at
Sir Henry Unton's marriage, c. 1596

MUSIC ON THE
SHAKESPEARIAN STAGE

BY

G. H. COWLING

Cambridge:
at the University Press
1913

Library of Congress Cataloging in Publication Data

Cowling, George Herbert, 1881-1946.
    Music in the Shakespearian stage.

    Reprint of the 1913 ed. published by University Press,
Cambridge.
    Bibliography: p.
    Includes index.
    1. Music—England—History and criticism. 2. Theater—
England—History and criticism. 3. Music in theaters.
I. Title.
[ML1731.2.C6   1976]   782.8'3'0942   74-24063
ISBN 0-404-12889-0

Reprinted from the edition of 1913, Cambridge,
First AMS edition published in 1976
Manufactured in the United States of America

AMS PRESS INC.
NEW YORK, N. Y.

PREFACE

WHEN my friend Professor Vaughan asked me if I had thought over any subject for a dissertation, I felt depressed. For I remembered the melancholy compilation that is expected from a student who sets out to take a degree in English Literature.

Whilst pondering over possible subjects, a music-teacher of my youth, the late Wallis Vincent, A.R.C.O. (one whom I admired greatly not only for his musicianship, which was considerable, but also for his delight in humorous poetry, his ready wit, and his genial kindness), lent me his manuscript of a popular lecture on "Shakespeare and Music." I was struck by the amount of fun he had got out of it, and foresaw that to make a deeper study of the subject would be to tread an interesting path. I made up my mind not to work the ground already appropriated by Mr E. W. Naylor and re-worked by Mr L. C. Elson, but to go further afield and describe the share taken by musicians in an Elizabethan play.

I drew up a scheme, was lucky enough to have it accepted, and proceeded to collect materials to make it into a dissertation. The result is the following little book. It does not assume to be more than a sketch, which at some future time I hope to enlarge. I should have liked to read and ransack every play of the period for material, but alas, I had not time enough for this.

Then why publish? I publish in order to report progress; but also because I think students of Shakespeare and musical historians will find in this essay much that is of interest, and something that is new.

The greatest regret I have is that Wallis Vincent should not read these pages. He saw the first draft of the MS. and used some of its material for his last lecture on "Shakespeare and Music." It was his appreciation that first led me to seek a publisher. To him I owe the greatest thanks, and to his dear memory I offer this acknowledgement.

In addition I thank Professor Moorman whose lectures on Shakespeare sealed my interest in the subject. My thanks are also due to Herbert Thompson, Esq., who readily furnished me with a preliminary bibliography; to Rev. W. H. Frere, who gave me a full account of "jubili"; to Rev. A. Hastings Kelk, who confirmed my suspicions about the source of Bale's canticles; to the readers of the Cambridge University Press, who pointed out, in addition to minor details, the great share which music had in the production of Italian drama of the period; and above all to Professor Vaughan, who, in addition to a sympathetic interest in the work, has been good enough to read the proofs.

One more note must be added. Since page 23 was written, M. Albert Feuillerat has shown (*Shakespeare Jahrbuch*, XLVIII. p. 81) that *Blackfriars* Theatre was founded as early as 1578 by Richard Farrant, the musician.

G. H. C.

LEEDS, 1912.

CONTENTS

LIST OF ILLUSTRATIONS

INTRODUCTION

THE following Essay is the outcome of curiosity—curiosity to know with what sort of stage-music and musical effect the Elizabethan dramatists produced their plays. It is an endeavour to do with the musical stage-directions what has already been done with those relating to other matters, namely, to collect them, and to force them to show their own conclusions. It endeavours to show what kinds of music were used during a play, and when and how the music was performed. Shakespeare's plays in First Folio and Quartos are the chief source of illustration, and other plays have been used as mines only that the ore extracted might illustrate the setting of a Shakespearian play. It concludes by attempting to estimate critically the artistic worth of music to the stage.

It may be objected that all this is purely antiquarian in its aim; but even if it were, it must not be assumed that all antiquarian research is of the dry-as-dust sort. It is highly important to obtain a clear idea of the conditions under which Elizabethan plays were produced, both for the light it throws upon the action of certain scenes, and also in order to clear away the old and false notions about the simplicity of the Elizabethan stage.

It has been assumed—the wish perhaps being father to the thought—that the drama of Shakespeare's age was a purely literary production. The decadence of poetic drama in our times has been attributed to a diseased craving for spectacle, scenic effect, and incidental music; and the perverse deduction has been drawn that the rise of drama in the Elizabethan age was owing to the fact that poetry was the only thing that mattered. "When Burbadge played, the stage was bare," sang Mr Austin Dobson, and more scholarly writers than he have failed to credit the importance of costumes, scenery, and music. Elizabethan drama has been called "a pure appeal to the ear." This is a quite inaccurate notion. It was also an appeal to the eye. The fact that moveable properties, and costumes other than Tudor were in use is shown by Henslowe's inventory of the goods, "aparell," and "properties for my Lord Admeralles men" at his playhouse *The Rose*[1]. An approach towards scenery is to be seen in the fact that the traverse was sometimes painted[2]. And the appeal to the ear was not made by poetry alone. There is a chain of evidence ranging from *Gorboduc* in 1562 and *Gammer Gurton's Needle* in 1566 to Prynne's *Histriomastix* in 1633 showing that music was a regular and important ingredient in the drama of Shakespeare's age. Thus Elizabethan drama was a sensuous appeal, not only to the ear with poetry and music, but to the eye with dress, properties, and painted scenes. Or, "to difference ourselves nearer," as Sir Thomas Browne would say, whilst the imagery of verse cast a glamour over the imaginative effect of the drama on the intellect and the emotions, there were music and colour for the senses.

[1] Supplement to *Henslowe's Diary*, ed. by J. P. Collier, Shakespeare Society (1845).

[2] "*Wife*. Now sweet lamb, what story is that painted on the cloth? The confutation of St Paul?" *Knight of the Burning Pestle*, Act II. Sc. 8.

The chief evidence to prove an extensive use of music is the mass of stage-directions in the texts of old plays. And the fact that musical stage-directions are not ideal, but were actually carried out, is substantiated by plenty of external evidence. For instance, Prynne has this syllogism in *Histriomastix* (Act V. Sc. 10):

"That which is alwaies accompanied with effeminate lust-provoking Musicke is doubtlesse inexpedient and un-lawfull unto Christians. But stage-plays are *alwayes* accompanied with such Musicke. Therefore they are doubtlesse inexpedient and unlawfull unto Christians." And his minor premise, says he, is "more then evident... *our Playhouses resounding alwayes with such voluptuous Melody.*"

Orazio Busino, who accompanied a Venetian embassy to the court of Elizabeth in 1618, visited *The Duchess of Malfi* at the *Fortune* theatre. "Some little amusement," he wrote in a letter, "may be derived...from the various interludes of instrumental music, and dancing, and singing[1]."

Further evidence is to be found in Henslowe's *Diary*, and especially in his inventory of the chattels of the Lord Admiral's Company, whom he employed at *The Rose* theatre during the year 1598[2]. When he took stock on March 10th and 13th of that year, he found the company in possession of three trumpets, one drum, one treble-viol,

---

[1] *Quarterly Review*, Vol. CII. pp. 416, and 423, note. One of the musical directions in the play is for a dance of madmen, "with music answerable thereto." (Act IV. Sc. 2.)

[2] As to the precise date of the tenure of *The Rose* theatre by the Lord Admiral's Company, authorities differ. Mr F. G. Fleay in *A Chronicle History of the London Stage* (1890), p. 145, gives the period as January 1598 to October 1600. Mr W. W. Greg, in *Henslowe's Diary* (1904), Part II. p. 187, says the Admiral's men were at *The Rose* from 11th October 1597 until 10th July 1600.

one bass-viol, one pandore, one cithern, one sackbut, three "tymbrells," and a chime of bells[1]. From time to time the company added more instruments to its stock. Henslowe's *Diary* contains the following entries:

(*a*) "Lent unto Thomas Dowton, the 10 of Novmbr 1598, to bye a sackebute of Marke Antoney for xxxxs."

Was this sackbut bought as a property for a play called "Mark Antony" or from another company playing a play with that name? It is difficult to say. The sackbut may have been bought as a property for a pre-Shakespearian *Julius Caesar*[2].

(*b*) "Lent unto Richard Jonnes the 22 of Desembr 1598 to bye a basse viall and other enstrements for the companey xxxxs."

(*c*) "Lent unto the company, the 6 of Febreary 1599 for to by a drome when to go into the country xjs vjd."

The company was going on tour, and needed drums and trumpets to herald its approach. Hence also the following:

(*d*) "Receaved of Mr Henshlowe this 7th of February 1599, the some of xxijs to buy 2 trumpettes xxijs. Robt. Shaa."

(*e*) "Lent unto Thomas Downton the 13 of July 1599, to bye enstrumentes for the Company, the some of xxxs."

Thus the players at *The Rose* theatre were in possession of enough musical instruments for a small band, and it is unlikely that all these instruments were simply stage-properties.

[1] From an inventory found by Malone amongst some loose papers of Henslowe's at Dulwich, but now lost. It is published by Collier in his *Henslowe's Diary*, Shakespeare Society (1845). Its authenticity is accepted by Mr Fleay, *Chronicle History of the London Stage* (1890), p. 115.

[2] Mr Greg thinks "Mark Antony" is the name of a character in a play, but also suggests that it may be the name of an Italian dealer in musical instruments. See *Henslowe's Diary*, ed. W. W. Greg, Vol. II. p. 199, note 158 (*a*).

And further proof is offered by the few theatre-plots that have come down to our day. The plot or " Platt " of a play was a large sheet affixed on the walls or doors of the tiring-room. It contained a list of cues for all the players, and in a side column was a running list of stage-directions. For example, the *Plott of the Firste Part of Tamar Cam* has the marginal note " sound sennet " when certain nobles are directed to enter, " sound flourish " when they leave the stage, and such directions as " sound," " alarum," " thunder," " wind horne," &c.[1] The *Platt of The Deade Man's Fortune* has the marginal direction " musique " between every act, but not at the beginning and end of the play[2]. The *Plat of The Battell of Alcazar* has the note " sound sennet " when a dumb-show enters, and has also directions for sounding trumpets during the play[3]. In addition to these external references to music in the playhouses, there are many references to theatrical musicians in contemporary tracts and pamphlets which will be noticed in a separate chapter[4].

From the internal evidence of the texts of plays it is plain that by its threefold use, in songs, in entertainments between the acts, and as an accompaniment to increase the emotional effect of verse, music played a great part in Elizabethan drama. The English had given music a share in their Mystery Plays. It held its own quite naturally in the Interlude and early Comedy, and was strong enough to force itself upon Elizabethan attempts to revive the classical drama, and thence into English Tragedy. Imitating their Italian masters, English musicians were beginning to break away from polyphonic music. The rules of counterpoint

---

[1] Malone's *Prolegomena*, Vol. III. Supplement.   [2] *Ibid.*
[3] *Bankside Shakespeare*, Vol. XX. Introduction.
[4] See Section VI.

were well understood, and were freely broken when necessary. The unaccompanied motets and madrigals of the latter half of the sixteenth century are so musicianly that the age has been called "the golden age of English music"; but with the introduction in the last decade of the century of solo-songs (or " Ayres ") accompanied by consorts of instruments, composers began to write definite melodies based on progressions of chords. In other words, the art of harmony came into being. At the same time composers began to forsake the old church-modes and to confine themselves to the major and minor modes.

In this decade the Italians were making their earliest attempts at Opera—a movement which did not spread to England until fifty years later—but the same craving for a mixed art compounded of poetry and music led to the gorgeous masques of Ben Jonson and his collaborators, and to popular song-plays like Nash's *Will Summer's Last Will and Testament.* Just as popular love of rough-and-tumble fun insisted on the retention of clowns and fools in Elizabethan drama, so love of music insisted that songs should be retained. Both were a heritage of Mystery and Interlude, but whilst the growing culture of the age did away with the fool, it raised the song to an artistic level, and made it a feature in almost every play. The lyrics of Shakespearian drama form one of its sweetest charms, and their surpassing beauty is due to the fact that they are the result of the strivings of generations of song-writers to surpass what had gone before.

CHAPTER I

MUSIC IN PRE-SHAKESPEARIAN DRAMA

Music in Mysteries—Latin canticles—English songs—John Heywood's influence—Songs in Interludes—*Ralph Roister Doister*—Influence of Italian drama—Dumb-shows—John Lyly—Court performances.

ENGLISH dramatic music took its beginnings from the antiphons and canticles of the medieval catholic church. The Mystery Plays—short dramas in popular verse dealing with scriptural incidents and legends of the saints—played by craft-gilds on certain festival days during the fifteenth and sixteenth centuries, drew quite naturally from the music of the church. Musicians played at times during their performance, and the plays contain antiphons, canticles, and a few lyrics—the earliest specimens of the English dramatic song[1].

It is impossible to give here a full list of references to music in the Mystery Plays; but we can get some notion of the share which music took by comparing the first play, *The Creation*, in existing series of gild-plays.

In the York play[2], a chorus of angels sings the canticles Te Deum laudamus, and Sanctus.

---

[1] Our mystery plays were paralleled in Italy by Sacre Rappresentazioni, from which Italian Oratorio took its rise. How did it happen that the golden age of English music produced no sacred musical drama?

[2] *York Mystery Plays*, ed. Miss Toulmin Smith (1885), pp. 2, 3.

In the Chester play, *The Creation and Fall*, minstrels play whilst God puts Adam and Eve in Paradise. After they have eaten the fruit, this direction is found, " Then Adam and Eve shall cover ther members with leaves, hyddinge themselves under they treeyes; then God shall speake, and mynstrelles playinge[1]." This attempt to add mystery to God's words by the use of music shows that the producers were well aware of the value of music for enhancing emotional effect.

In the Norwich play[2], *The Creacion of Eve, &c.*, there is a direction that music shall be played when Adam and Eve are driven out of Paradise. Adam and Eve then sing an English lyric :

" Wythe dolorous sorowe, we may wayle and wepe
    Both nyght and daye in sory sythys full depe," &c.

But by far the greater number of songs in the Mysteries are church canticles, which would be sung to their accustomed melodies, and known to the church-goers who heard them therein sung. The introduction of songs in English was a further step away from holy church, and a first step towards the songs of Shakespeare.

In the Coventry *Creation*[3], as in the York play, a choir of angels sings a part of Te Deum laudamus, in this case the lines from " Tibi omnes angeli " to " Sanctus, Dominus Deus Sabaoth."

The Towneley play of *The Creation, &c.*, has twelve leaves missing[4], so that it is impossible to say whether musicians were employed. This series has but few stage-directions, yet it would be rash to draw thence the conclusion

---

[1] *Chester Plays*, Shakespeare Society (1843), pp. 23, 30. This particular play was done appropriately enough by the Drapers.

[2] *Non-Cycle Mystery Plays*, Early English Text Society (1909), p. 10.

[3] *Coventry Mysteries*, Shakespeare Society (1841), p. 20.

[4] *Towneley Plays*, Early English Text Society (1897), p. 9.

that the Towneley plays were performed without music. For example, the second *Shepherds' Play* ends with the Yorkshire shepherds bringing toys for the holy child to Bethlehem. Their last words are—

> *First Shepherd.* What grace we have fun.
> *Second Shepherd.* Come forth, now are we won.
> *Third Shepherd.* To sing are we bun.
> Let take on loft."

—And it is likely that they finished their show with a carol, for in a corresponding Coventry *Nativity*[1] play the shepherds sing a delightful carol :

> "As I outrode this enderes night,
> Of three jolly shepherds I saw a sight,
> And all about their fold a star shone bright ;
> They sang Terli, Terlow ;
> So merrily the shepherds their pipes can blow."

And another charming carol is to be found towards the end of the same play which deals with *The Slaughter of the Innocents.* The mothers sing a lullaby to their children lamenting Herod's decree, with the burden—

> "Lully, lulla, thou tiny little child ;
> By, by, lullay, lullay, thou little tiny child ;
> By, by, lully lullay."

It is impossible to overestimate the importance of these folksongs. They paved the way, as we have said, for the lyric of later drama, but even greater was their influence on music. The church canticles such as Ave Maria[2], Veni Creator Spiritus[3], Gloria[4], Salvum me fac, Domine[5] (Psalm

---

[1] The Coventry Nativity Play (from the text of Robert Croo, 1534) "*Everyman*" *with other Interludes.* Everyman's Library.

[2] In York, " The Annunciation."

[3] In York, " The Baptism of Jesus."

[4] In Towneley, "Shepherds' Plays," and in Coventry, " Nativity Play."

[5] In Chester, " The Deluge."

lxix), Exultet coelum laudibus[1], Stella coeli extirpavit[2],
and Te Deum laudamus, which were sung in certain
Mysteries, were adorned with long jubili or "runs." Thus
in the Latin songs from the York Mysteries, "mea," in one
place, is sung on a run of twenty-one notes, and "surge"
to nineteen[3]. As long as these dramatic songs were in
Latin, the fact that jubili obscured the sense did not
matter. For though perhaps the language was not understood, yet the meaning was, because the canticles were
well known to all who attended church. But with the
introduction of English words these over-elaborations
had to go. Henceforth melodies must be rhythmic, and
suited to the words. Their runs and gracenotes were not
allowed to interfere with the meaning of the song. The
rise of harmony in the last half of the sixteenth century
finally killed jubili. Composers then decorated and elaborated their music with harmony rather than by adorning
the melody, and aimed at expressing the meaning of
the song in music. Thomas Morley's *Plaine and Easie
Introduction to Practicall Musicke* (1597) gives instruction
"how to dispose your musicke according to the nature of
the words which you are therein to expresse." "If you
have a grave matter, apply a grave kinde of musicke to it ;
if a merry subject, you must make your musicke also
merrie." He tells how to "signifie hardnesse" by using
whole-notes, and "a lamentable passion" with half-notes ;
the goal being to have "as it were an harmonical consent
betwixt the matter and the musick."

The direct successors of Mysteries were the longer and

---

[1] In Coventry, "The Barrenness of Anna."

[2] In Coventry, "The Adoration of the Shepherds."

[3] Five songs from the York Mysteries. Ashburnham MS. 137, leaf 238.
Supplement to Miss Toulmin Smith's *York Mystery Plays*.

more elaborate scriptural plays which held popular favour until the end of the sixteenth century. Greene and Lodge's play, *A Looking Glass for London and England* (1594), and Peele's *David and Bethsabe* (ca. 1599) were perhaps the last. Earlier scriptural plays show the transition clearly in the nature of their songs. John Bale (1495—1563), protestant Bishop of Ossory, was the author of *A Brefe Comedy of Johan Baptyste* and *A Tragedy of God's Promises* (1538). The latter treats in seven acts of the woeful afflictions of seven characters taken from the Bible. Each of the seven sings to express his faith in God's promises. The songs chosen are the Advent antiphons of the pre-reformation English liturgy,—O Sapientia, O Adonai, O Radix Jesse, O Clavis David, O Oriens splendor, O Rex Gentium, and O Emmanuel—sung not in due order, but distributed with fitting regard for the seven tragic heroes. Thus, Noah, on seeing the rainbow, sings O Oriens splendor. John the Baptist, laid in prison, sings O Clavis David. The stage-directions indicate that a "chorus" of instrumentalists accompanied the singers, but the organ seems to have taken their place at Kilkenny on August 20th, 1553, when "the yonge men in the forenone played a tragedy of *God's Promises in the Old Lawe*, at the Market Crosse, with Organs plainge and songes very aptely[1]."

These antiphons are a link connecting with the Latin canticles of the Mysteries. But the English song persisted. In *The History of Jacob and Esau* (1557)[2], along with English canticles, there is a humorous folksong with the burden,

"For young doth it prick, that will be a thorn."

[1] "The Vocacyon of Johan Bale," quoted by E. F. Rimbault in his Introduction to *Bonduca* (1842), p. 6.

[2] Dodsley-Hazlitt collection. (*A Select collection of Old English Plays*, pub. Reeves and Turner, London, 1874), Vol. II. p. 234.

But whilst popular lyrics hardly held their ground in scriptural plays, they were swept along the high road towards perfection owing to the invention of a new type of play by a court musician named John Heywood. In his early youth (ca. 1515) Heywood left Oxford to join the court of Henry VIII as a singer. There he spent his life as musician and playwright until, on the accession of Elizabeth, being too devout a Catholic to remain, he went abroad. When Heywood began his career, the plays in fashion at court were the so-called Moralities,—allegorical and didactic plays dealing not with real persons but with symbolical and abstract characters. Persons such as Truth, Justice, Peace, Mercy, Mankind, the seven Deadly Sins, Vice, and the like, carried on scholastic disputations and fought exemplary battles in which virtue always won, and vice was driven into Hell. They were played on elaborate stages; but from the nature of the plays, singing was rare, though it is not impossible that minstrels played during their performance[1].

The advance which Heywood made was that his persons stand for a class such as the Pedlar, or the Priest, instead of abstractions like Truth, Youth, Mercy and the rest. Although his Interludes lack plot, and are simply discussions like the Morality plays, yet the chord of human interest struck by him made the introduction of songs possible. The fact too that he was by profession a musician, and one of a large band of musician-retainers at court, doubtless had its influence on the association of music with his kind of early drama. It is on record that in 1521, £5 was paid "To John Haywoode synger wages[2]."

---

[1] It is worth noting that *La Rappresentazione del' Anima e del Corpo* (Rome, 1600) was a Morality play set to music.

[2] "The Kynges boke of payments," quoted by Collier, *Annals*, I. p. 77.

In 1526 he had risen to be "player of the virginals" and received £6. 13s. 4d. quarterly[1]. In 1538, for some reason, his quarterly salary had fallen to £2. 10s. 0d[2], but Edward VI raised his fee to £50 a year[3], and Mary continued it at the same rate[4].

To Heywood also belongs the credit of leading up to a song with fitting dialogue. For example, his *Interlude of the Four Ps* deals with the chance meeting of a Pardoner, a Palmer, a 'Pothecary and a Pedlar, who strive to tell the wildest lying tale. When all are met, the 'Pothecary enquires if the Pedlar can sing—

> "*Pothecary.* I pray you tell me, can you sing?
> *Pedlar.* Sir, I have some sight in singing.
> *Pothecary.* But is your breast anything sweet[5]?"

Then they sing, but, as is the case with most early plays, the words of the song are not given. They may have sung a part-song, or a madrigal, for the Madrigalists began their art in England before 1530. In that year Wynkyn de Worde printed the first English song-book entitled, *XX Songes; IX of IIII partes and XI of thre partes*, although the best English madrigals were not written until just after 1600, by Wilbye, Gibbons, and their fellows.

Heywood's kind of Interlude did not altogether shut out plays of an ethical and controversial nature, but thenceforward songs were common in both Morality and Interlude, and they were given even to personifications. For example, in *Lusty Juventus*[6] (ca. 1550) Hypocrisy and Abhominable

---

[1] "A Booke of Wages, 17 Hen. VIII," quoted by Collier, *Annals*, I. p. 96.
[2] Collier, *Annals*, I. p. 119.
[3] Burney, *History of Music*, Vol. III. p. 5.   [4] Collier, *Annals*, I. p. 165.
[5] Dodsley-Hazlitt collection, Vol. I. p. 353.   "Breast" means chest-voice. Cf. *Twelfth Night* (Act II. Sc. 3), where Aguecheek exclaims, "By my troth, the fool hath an excellent breast."
[6] Dodsley-Hazlitt collection, Vol. II. p. 88.

Living sing a merry song with a burden " Report me to you."
In *The Interlude of the Four Elements*[1] (1519) musicians
sing and dance before Sensual Appetite. An interesting
direction "if ye list ye may bring in a disguising" occurs
in the introduction. If a "disguising" or masque were
brought in, instrumentalists must have been needed to
play for the songs and dances. The direction also shows
that Shakespeare's introduction of masques into his later
plays was no new thing[2]. *An Interlude of Wealth and
Health*[3] (1557) begins with Wealth and Health singing
together "a ballat of two parts," and later in the play
Liberty "entereth with a song." *Impatient Poverty*[4] (1560)
has the stage-direction " Here Misrule singeth without
coming in." It was common in late Elizabethan drama
to direct that a song be sung " Within," and herein it
is manifest that the custom had a precedent in elder
drama.

About half way through the sixteenth century an effort
was made to wean drama from its didactic setting. Moral
and scriptural characters were put into the background,
and the play turned on a dramatic situation. Religious
songs were put aside, and songs of a humorous kind called
for. The Morality-Tragedy *Appius and Virginia*[5] (? 1563)
contains comic songs sung by a row of persons, of whom
each sings one verse. Early comedies, like *Tom Tyler and*

---

[1] Dodsley-Hazlitt collection, Vol. I. pp. 5, 46.

[2] Of the instances referred to, only one, namely the masque in *The
Tempest*, is a masque in the strict sense of the word. But the supernatural
visions in *Pericles*, *Cymbeline*, and *Henry VIII* have manifestly elements in
common with the masque.

[3] *Lost Tudor Plays*, ed. J. S. Farmer for the Early English Drama Society
(1907), p. 275.

[4] *Ibid.* p. 332.

[5] Dodsley-Hazlitt collection, Vol. IV.

his Wife[1] (ca. 1560), and *The Nice Wanton* (1560)[2], usually have several humorous songs; the former contains seven.

Nicholas Udall's *Ralph Roister Doister*[3] (ca. 1550), though entitled an Interlude, is really the first extant English comedy. It contains no hint of allegorical figures. Its characters are not much more convincingly sketched than Heywood's, but they are skilfully put in a comic situation and the knot is unravelled in real comedy fashion. The plot hinges on Dame Custance's wooing by the vainglorious Ralph, and the final triumph of her affianced Garvin Goodluck. It contains several comic songs, introduced in Heywood's manner by fitting dialogue, as for example the song in Act I. Sc. 3 sung by Dame Custance's maidens. The song "Whoso to marry a minion wife" in Act I. Sc. 4 is introduced thus—

"*R. Roister.*   Go to it, sirs, lustily.
M. Mumble.   Pipe up a merry note,
              Let me hear it played, I will foot it for a groat."

This proves that the accompaniment was played by musicians[4] and moreover that the time was a dance measure—a great advance on the plain-song carols and canticles of the Mysteries. At the beginning of Act II Ralph's servant soliloquises that "with every woman" his master is "in some love's pang," and that he serenades them with sonnets and ballads of his own making, accompanied by lute, recorder, and gittern.

In Act III. Sc. 3 Ralph is dying of unrequited love. His parasite Merrygreeke intones what the stage-direction

---

[1] *Anonymous Plays*, 2nd Series, ed. J. S. Farmer for the Early English Drama Society (1906).

[2] Dodsley-Hazlitt collection, Vol. II.   [3] *Ibid.* Vol. III.

[4] Actors similarly address musicians in *Gammer Gurton's Needle*, end of Act II; *Ralph Roister Doister*, end of Act III. Sc. 3; and in *The Knight of the Burning Pestle*.

calls "The Psalmody"—a lament for Ralph in which he calls on Ralph's servants to begin "some part of his funerals." Five servants then sing a round in imitation of the chiming of bells. Under the influence of this doleful music Ralph recovers and calls for musicians. When Merrygreeke brings them he says, "Come sirs, let us sing to win my dear love Custance." Then he sings, "I mun be married a Sunday." The play ends with antiphons sung by the principal characters equivalent in intention to our custom of playing or singing "God save the King" at the end of an entertainment.

Gammer Gurton's Needle[1], a comedy similar in that it deals with village life, but coarser in tone, shows a corresponding use of music. At the end of Act I occurs the famous old song, "I cannot eat but little meat," and the fact that music was played between the acts is indicated at the end of Act II, where Diccon says to the musicians—

"In the meantime, fellows, pipe up your fiddles: I say take them
And let your friends hear such mirth as ye can make them."

Both the foregoing plays were produced by scholars. *Ralph Roister Doister* is supposed to have been played at Eton, and *Gammer Gurton's Needle* was played at Christ's College, Cambridge, in 1566. And the more elaborate use of music in these comedies, and in the Interludes played in the houses of princes and noblemen, than in the popular Mysteries, points to a more cultured audience with ready access to capable musicians.

In the decade of the sixties, the influence of Italian Renaissance drama began to manifest itself in England, particularly in the plays produced by the benchers of the Inns of Court. "Generally speaking," says M. Romain

[1] Dodsley-Hazlitt collection, Vol. III.

Rolland[1], "no drama whether classic or neo-classic was played in Italy in the XVIth century without music."... "The text was spoken, but there were many songs, and dumb-shows were considerably developed." The typical Renaissance English comedy *The Supposes* (1566), by George Gascoigne, contains no songs[2], but the manuscript of *The Bugbears* (ca. 1565) contains four songs, the music for two of which still exists[3].

English writers of Renaissance tragedy copied an Italian form of art which came into being ca. 1500—the *intermedio* or pantomime with music. *Intermedi* were staged both as a distinct kind of drama and as entr'actes in tragedy and comedy[4]. Under their influence our Renaissance dramatists introduced a "dumb-show" accompanied by music at the beginnings of each act in order to illustrate the plot. Sometimes the persons in this musical pantomime were allegorical, sometimes they were drawn from the dramatis personae. The effect of these spectacles on the audience must have been to whet curiosity, something like a charade.

As a typical example, this is the "Order of the Dumb-show before the First Act" of *Gorboduc*[5], written by Norton and Sackville, and produced by gentlemen of the Inner Temple at Whitehall on January 18, 1562.— "First, the music of violins began to play, during which

---

[1] *Musiciens d'Autrefois* (*L'opéra avant l'opéra*), by M. Romain Rolland, publ. Hachette (1912), p. 39.

[2] Its original, *Gli Suppositi* of Ariosto, was played at the Vatican in March 1518 with entr'actes played by fifes, cornmuses, cornets, viols, lutes and organ. See *Musiciens d'Autrefois*, p. 37.

[3] *Early Plays from the Italian*, ed. Bond, p. 154.

[4] See article by O. G. Sonneck in *Musical Antiquary*, Oct. 1911.

[5] *Roister Doister and Gorboduc*, ed. W. D. Cooper. Shakespeare Society, 1847.

came in upon the stage six wild men, clothed in leaves. Of whom the first bare on his neck a faggot of small sticks, which they all, both severally and together, assayed with all their strength to break, but it could not be broken by them." The "order" continues that they tore the sticks apart and then easily broke them. The moral of this dumb-show is that disunion makes weakness—a moral exemplified in this play, wherein King Gorboduc divides his kingdom betwixt his two sons, by the manifold woes that ensue. In *Gorboduc*, cornets played for the dumb-show before Act II; flutes (then considered a mournful instrument) accompanied the dumb-show before Act III, for it contained a murder; hautboys played for the fourth; and drums and flutes for the fifth dumb-show, which betokens wars and tumults. "First, the drums and flutes began to sound, during which there came forth upon the stage a company of harquebussiers, and of armed men, all in order of battle. These, after their pieces discharged, and that the armed men had three times marched about the stage, departed, and then the drums and flutes did cease."

Tancred and Gismunda[1] (1568—1572), another Inner Temple play, contains similar dumb-shows. Its plot is based on the novel in the *Decamerone* which treats of the tragic love of Princess Sigismunda for the squire Guiscard. Before the third act "the hautboys sounded a lofty almain" whilst Guiscard and Gismunda danced. Before the fourth act was a dumb-show of the king spying on the lovers' embracements, accompanied by "a consort of sweet musick." A dead-march was played before the fifth act to prepare the audience for the tragic ending. This Renaissance tragedy also contained a song. Gismunda and her maidens sang at the end of the second scene. "Cantant" says the

[1] Dodsley-Hazlitt collection, Vol. VII.

stage-direction of the transcriber, but "Quae mihi cantio nondum occurrit."

In Gascoigne's *Jocasta*[1] (1566) there are similar dumb-shows accompanied by music of viols, cytherns, pandores, flutes, cornets, trumpets, drums, fifes, and still-pipes; and the same feature is to be found in *The Misfortunes of Arthur*[2], a play produced in 1588 for the delectation of Queen Elizabeth by various members of Gray's Inn. It was such a dumb-show that Shakespeare introduced into *Hamlet*, and his intent was no doubt to make the play within the play seem archaic to his audience; for when English tragedy made a fresh beginning from the early chronicle-plays dealing with stories of English kings, dumb-shows were discarded.

Yet another sort of play produced for court amusement were the comedies of John Lyly (1554?—1606), a university scholar, who, to use the words of Gabriel Harvey, "hath not played the Vicemaster of Poules and the Foolemaster of the Theater for naught." They are plays of five acts, with a classical or mythological fable written in prose tinged with the fashionable Euphuism of the day. The influence of the Interlude is there in the shape of symbolic characters and allegorical meaning. Lyly was probably assistant master of the choir-boys of St Paul's, and his comedies were acted before the Queen by them or by the Children of the Chapel Royal. In his plays are technical references to singing and musical instruments which go to prove that Lyly had an intimate knowledge of music[3]. Songs are introduced, usually at the end of scenes; but,

[1] Gascoigne's Works. Cambridge University Press, 1907, Vol. I. p. 246.

[2] Dodsley-Hazlitt collection, Vol. IV.

[3] Cf. *Campaspe*, Act IV. 3, 20 ; *Endimion*, Act III. 4, 1 ; *Midas*, Prologue, Act III. 2, 85 and Act IV. 1 ; *Mother Bombie*, Act V. 3.

with the exception of two songs in *The Woman in the Moone*, the songs that appear in copies of the Folio edition of 1632 are probably not by Lyly[1]. Like Heywood, he often leads up to the introduction of a song by suitable dialogue. He gives no musical directions in his plays, but as they were played on the same kind of stage as the court Interludes and the entertainments provided by the Inns of Court, it is likely that viols, lutes of various kinds, flutes, and virginals accompanied the songs.

The establishment of the Children of the Chapel Royal (ca. 1561) consisted of eight viols, three drums, two flutes, three virginals, seven " musition straungers " of whom four were "Brethren Venetions "—probably the Bassano brothers —and eight players of Interludes[2]. The entrance of the Queen was probably heralded at these court entertainments by flourishes of drums and trumpets. All the Tudor monarchs kept a large band of trumpet and sackbut players. Henry VIII had fifteen trumpeters and ten sackbutists[3]. In 1571 Elizabeth maintained eighteen trumpeters and six sackbut players[4]. She delighted in the sound of drums and trumpets. Every day the signal for dinner was given by twelve trumpets and a pair of drums who " made the hall ring for half an hour together[5]."

The lists of Queen Elizabeth's household musicians have been published recently. The numbers vary slightly owing to deaths and the engagement of new musicians. In the year cited by Mr Barclay Squire[6], the musicians and players consisted of seventeen trumpeters, six sackbuts,

---

[1] See article by W. W. Greg, *Modern Language Review*, Vol. I.

[2] Collier, *Annals*, Vol. I. p. 178.

[3] *Ibid*. pp. 94, 95.   [4] *Ibid*. pp. 201, 202.

[5] Chappell, *Popular Music of the Olden Time*, 1859, Vol. I. p. 245, note.

[6] *Musical Antiquary*, beginning Oct. 1909. Mr Barclay Squire's list of wages is in the number for January, 1910.

three drumsleds (*i.e.* drummers), two players on the flute, two lutanists, one rebeck, eight viols, two harpers, two players on the virginals, two makers of instruments, eight singers, six singing children, nine minstrels, eight Interlude players, and seven "musician strangers" including the four Venetian brethren mentioned above.   There seems to have been a reduction in the number of household musicians towards the end of the reign.   The eighteen trumpeters were retained, but the sackbuts were reduced to two.   The names of the trumpeters are always English, but for the other instruments of music Italian names are prevalent.

With this huge band of musicians at Elizabeth's court —the centre of the fashionable and best society of the age in England—it is not surprising that music became popular in the theatre.   Italian influence guided its use in the court entertainments, and the court entertainments in their turn influenced the private theatres.   With an aristocracy fond of music, and accustomed to play and listen to music and song, music in the theatre was almost as inevitable in England as in Italy.

CHAPTER II

AN ELIZABETHAN STAGE AND ITS MUSIC

Erection of theatres—Public and private theatres—The Elizabethan
stage—Position of musicians—Music-rooms—Music on the
platform—Armies—Processions—Masquers—Music "Within"—
Music on the balcony—"Infernal music."

UP to the year 1576 all the divers kinds of English
drama were acted on improvised stages. The Mysteries
were played on pageants erected by the craft-gilds, the
Scripture-plays on temporary platforms erected in inn-yards
and public squares, the Moralities and Interludes in the
halls of nobles, and the pseudo-classical Tragedies in the
halls of the Inns of Court, and at the Palace of Whitehall.
They were all occasional productions performed on the day
of some festival or merry-making, and under such conditions, a highly finished performance was hardly possible.
But in that year the first public theatres were built—*The
Theatre* and *The Curtain* in Shoreditch—soon after to be
followed by *The Rose* on Bankside, and the *Newington
Butts* Theatre. Their popularity was immediate, and by
the turn of the century, half a score theatres were built,
including *The Globe* and *The Swan* in the liberty of the
Clink on Bankside, and *The Fortune* in Cripplegate.

Their musical importance lies in the fact that with the
establishment of a standard stage, a standard use of stage-
music came into being. Of course there were variations in the

Plate I

The *Fortune* Theatre

construction of each theatre, and it is most likely that every theatre had its own arrangement of musical details; but the stage-directions of dramas played at these theatres are sufficiently uniform to allow one to get a general notion of the share which music took in a dramatic show during the age of Shakespeare. Thus, a song was almost a *sine qua non*, and was far more regular in its presence than a fool or a clown. There is evidence to show that jigs and dances were performed during the intervals between the acts. And some musical directions, such for example as " a flourish of trumpets " at the entrance of a noble person, or the introduction of drums and colours in the van of a stage-army, occur with clockwork regularity.

In 1596[1], on the site of Playhouse Yard behind the *Times* newspaper office, *Blackfriars* Theatre was opened. It was called a " private " theatre, the epithet implying that in construction it was like the private theatres of Whitehall or the Inns of Court. The public theatres were built something like a travelling circus, that is to say they consisted of a ring or arena surrounded by grandstands, save at one side where the stage jutted out into the ring. The stage and grandstands were sheltered by a thatched roof, but the ring was open to the sky. Unlike the public theatres, *Blackfriars* and its rival theatre *Whitefriars* were halls containing a stage where performances took place by candle-light. The fact that these " private " theatres were leased to the Children of the Chapel Royal, and the Children of the Revels, accounts for the elaborate music in the plays performed there, and doubtless the managers of the " aery of children " saw to it that the excellence of their music was an attraction big enough to outweigh their deficiencies as matured actors.

[1] 1596 Albright, 1597 Fleay, 1596 Collier.

Turning now to discuss the construction of Elizabethan and Jacobean stages, it is necessary to point out that they projected much further into the auditorium than do modern stages. On our stage, action is seen as in a box with a missing side. Their stage was a pageant, and their acting could be viewed as well from the sides as from the front of the stage. Rising from the midst of this platform were two beams which supported a sounding-board or " heavens," under which on occasion a hoist was let down for the entrance of supernatural personae. Under the " heavens," behind the two beams was an inner chamber, closed when required by a curtain or " traverse," and roofed by the players' tiring-house which opened upon a balcony. At the sides of the stage were doors. A door opened upon the balcony, and there was a way passing through the traverse and the inner chamber to the back of the stage.

Thus there were three parts of the stage where action could be carried on—the platform, the inner chamber, and the balcony. In many plays action did take place in all. three parts of the stage. For instance in *Romeo and Juliet*, Juliet's balcony would be the balcony before the tiring-house, and the inner chamber would be the tomb of the Capulets[1]. The position of the musicians is a matter of conjecture, but the evidence seems to show that in early public theatres where there was scarcely any music save drums and trumpets, no space for musicians was provided. Later (? ca. 1600—1605) one " room " or box was reserved for them at the side of the stage in all theatres, probably above one of the side doors.

To take the evidence in due order. Marston's *Malcontent* was taken by the company of actors called His

---

[1] An article by William Archer entitled " The Fortune Theatre 1600 " in *Shakespeare Jahrbuch* XLIV; also *The Shakesperian Stage*, by Victor Albright.

Plate II

The *Globe* Theatre

(*As reconstructed at Earl's Court,* 1912)

Majesty's Servants from the Children of the Chapel Royal who were acting at *Blackfriars*—a private theatre, where elaborate music was played—as a counterstroke for their theft of *The Spanish Tragedy*. *The Malcontent* was played at *The Globe* in 1604 with an induction by Webster[1]. In this induction, Sly (an actor) is made to ask—

"What are your additions?"

and Burbadge answers—

"Sooth, not greatly needful; only as your salad to your great feast, to entertain a little more time, and to abridge the not received custom of music in our theatre[2]."

Here is proof that music was not in regular use at *The Globe* in 1604, though there must have been trumpets and drums to play the flourishes and alarums needed for the historical plays that were staged there.

A similar state of things probably might have been found at *The Swan*, a neighbouring theatre on Bankside. A sketch of this theatre, made by John De Witt who visited London in 1596, exists in the Royal Library at Berlin. It shows a theatre-interior like the type we have described, save that there is no inner chamber under the balcony[3], which means probably nothing more than that Elizabethan theatres were not built on a uniform model. In De Witt's sketch, the seats at the immediate left-hand side of the stage are designated "orchestra," but it is a moot point whether or not they were occupied by musicians. Cotgrave's Dictionary (1611) defines "Orchestre" as "The senators' or noblemen's places in a theatre

[1] F. G. Fleay, *Chronicle of the English Drama*, Vol. II. p. 78.

[2] The last clause is very difficult to interpret, but it seems to indicate that the "additions" to the dialogue were intended to take the place of the music at *Blackfriars*.

[3] A picture of the *Red Bull* theatre, in the frontispiece to *Kirkman's Drolls* (1672), shows the traverse clearly. A reproduction is to be seen in the *Mermaid* edition of Thomas Heywood's plays.

between the stage and the common seats. Also the stage itself[1]." And it seems highly probable that De Witt's orchestra was simply the stage-box of that time, for which the highest fee for admission was paid[2]. But some time between 1596 and 1612, a music-room came into existence at *The Swan* theatre. Middleton's *Chaste Maid in Cheap-side* played there in 1612[3] has the stage-direction " A sad song in the Music Room." De Witt's sketch also shows a trumpeter standing at a window above "the heavens" and blowing his instrument whilst the play is in progress on the stage. This is surely an inaccuracy. It is unlikely that flourishes on the entrance of noble personae were played from the topmost story, because of the difficulty of giving the cue to the trumpeter. He must have stood near one of the doors leading on to the platform. Is it possible that the sketch is merely the recollection of a visit made to *The Swan* playhouse, and that the author depicted both the trumpet prelude and the play in progress?

But if it be true that the early Bankside playhouses had no special place reserved for the music, it was not true of all theatres. Certainly the private theatres possessed " music-rooms." A plan of the King's *Masquing House* at Whitehall made by Inigo Jones exists in the British Museum, which shows the " music-house " at the side of the stage[4]. Malone similarly records : " The band, which, I believe did not consist of more than eight or ten performers, sat (as I have been told by a very ancient stage-veteran, who had his information from Bowman, the contemporary of Betterton) in an upper balcony over what is now called

---

[1] Quoted by Malone, *Prolegomena*, Vol. III. p. 114, note 1.

[2] See article by W. J. Lawrence, *Shakespeare Jahrbuch* XLIV. p. 46.

[3] Fleay, *Chronicle of the English Drama*, Vol. II. p. 96.

[4] Lansdowne MSS. No. 1171, *Inigo Jones' Plans for Masques at Whitehall*, Fo. 10.

Plate III

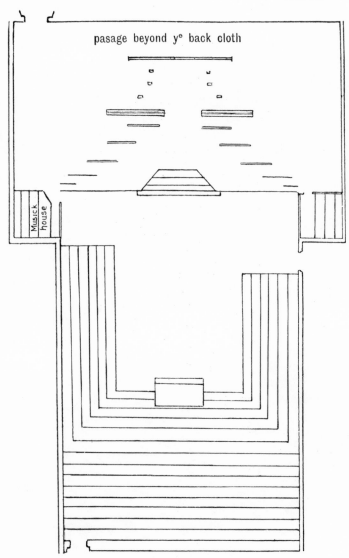

pasage beyond yᵉ back cloth

Musick house

Inigo Jones' Plan of the Masquing House at Whitehall

the stage-box[1]." Marston's *Sophonisba*, done at *Blackfriars* in 1606, has the direction "A short song to soft music *above*," which implies an upper room of some kind.

In the case of a theatre which had no special music-room, the tiring-house behind the balcony seems to have been used. The "not received custom of music" at *The Globe* seems to have been relaxed in 1604 for the production of the Marston-Webster *Malcontent* in favour of a band of wind-instruments. The play begins with this direction: "The vilest out-of-tune music being heard, enter Bilioso and Prepasso," followed by this dialogue:

" *Pietro*: Where breathes that music?
> *Bilioso*: The discord rather than the music is heard from the malcontent Malevole's chamber."

Malevole appears "above," on the balcony, which implies that the band were playing in the tiring-room; but in the same play they also played within the inner chamber, for in Act II. Sc. 3 the direction "Music within" occurs, and this dialogue:

> "*Bianca*: Hark! Music!
> *Maquerelle*: Peace! 'tis i' the duchess' bed-chamber."

A song is sung within the chamber, and then Ferneze rushes through the traverse on to the stage and is murdered. "Confirmatory evidence is found in the third act of *The Late Lancashire Witches* (1634), as acted at *The Globe*. Quite unconscious of their offence, the bewitched musicians have been plaguing the wedding guests with unearthly discords. Each, in fact, has been playing a different tune. They are asked to try again. 'I, and let's see your faces,' says Doughty, 'that you play fairly with us'; and then follows the direction, 'Musitians shew themselves above[2].'"

---

[1] Malone, *Prolegomena*, Vol. III. p. 111, 1821 edn.

[2] W. J. Lawrence's article "Music in the Elizabethan Theatre," *Shakespeare Jahrbuch* XLIV. p. 47.

At *Whitefriars*, where Beaumont and Fletcher's *Knight of the Burning Pestle* was played (ca. 1610)[1], the music-room was at the side of the stage. At the end of Act II the Citizen and his wife are left alone on the stage. He has given the players money to bring in "the waits of Southwark" and they are expecting to hear the reedy music of hautboys. Instead of that they hear viols.

"*Wife*: The fiddlers go again, husband.
  Citizen: Ay, Nell; but this is scurvy music. I gave the whoreson
        gallows money, and I think he has not got me the waits
        of Southwark: if I hear em not anon, I'll twinge him by
        the ears."

From this it is clear that they could hear but not see the musicians, which would indicate that the band was aloft in a side box; for had they been in the centre of the stage, either in the inner chamber or on the balcony, the Citizen and his Nell could have seen them.

The private theatre where the Children of Paul's played (ca. 1600) possessed two music-rooms. *The Second Part of Antonio and Mellida*[2] (Act V. Sc. 2) has this direction: "While the measure is dancing, Andrugio's ghost is placed betwixt the music-houses," and later in the same scene: "The curtains being drawn, exit Andrugio"; but it is not clear whether the music-rooms were situated on the level of the stage, or on the level of the balcony. The use of music-rooms lasted into Restoration Drama. Killigrew's *Parson's Wedding* (1664) has references to personae being "above in the musick room," and to fiddlers playing in the tiring-room[3]. Pepys also records a visit to the *Red Bull*

---

[1] F. G. Fleay, *Chronicle of the English Drama*, Vol. I. p. 182.
[2] See title-page of the play. "Antonios Reuenge. The second part. As it hath beene sundry times acted, by the children of Paules," &c. 1602.
[3] Cited by W. J. Lawrence, *Shakespeare Jahrbuch* XLIV. p. 49.

playhouse on March 23rd 1661, when there was "so much disorder, among others, in the musique room, the boy that was to sing a song not singing it right, his master fell about his eares and beat him so that it put the whole house in an uproare." Musicians were first brought in front of the stage to the place we know as "orchestra" by Davenant, when he produced Dryden's version of Shakespeare's *Tempest* in 1667[1].

To sum up. It seems likely that the first public theatres had no special places reserved for musicians. The drummers and trumpeters they employed moved about from stage to balcony and turret as they were required. Later theatres were built with a music-room at the side to house the musicians that were needed to play for dances and songs; and then, when music had become an absolutely necessary attraction, the older theatres (including those on Bankside) fell into line, and housed their musicians in the tiring-house behind the balcony. Probably the Paul's boys' theatre was exceptional, and the regular use was to build one box called the music-room at the side of the balcony.

But it must not be supposed that the musicians remained in their pen like a modern orchestra. On the contrary, every part of the stage used by players was also used by the musicians. They were even sent down to the cellarage like Hamlet's father's ghost to conjure supernatural effects from beneath the platform. Let us turn to examine how the different parts of the stage were used by Elizabethan playwrights for musical effect.

First, the platform. When an army came on the stage, it was accompanied by "drum and colours," or in other words, by a drummer and an ensign. The following

---

[1] Collier, *Annals of the Stage*, Vol. III. p. 448. Also Malone, *Prolegomena*, Vol. III. p. 114, note 1, ed. 1821.

directions taken chiefly from historical plays staged between 1590 and 1600 give good evidence of this.

Titus Andronicus begins, "Flourish. Enter the Tribunes and Senators
aloft. And then enter Saturninus and his followers at one
door, and Bassianus and his followers at the other, with
Drum and Colours."

This interesting stage-direction describes the stage of a
public theatre so clearly that it scarcely needs comment.
After a flourish of trumpets, the Tribunes and Senators
came out of the tiring-room and lined the balcony over-
looking the platform; and whilst the army of Bassianus,
provided with a drummer beating a rhythmic march, filed
out of one of the side doors to take up its position on the
platform, the followers of Saturninus entered in procession
from the other.   Probably only one drum was used.

Peele's *David and Bethsabe*.   "Enter Joab, Abisai, Urias, and others,
with Drum and Ensign."

The True Tragedy of Richard, Duke of York begins, "Enter Richard
Duke of York," &c. "with Drum and Soldiers."

Ibid.   "Enter the Earl of Warwick, Montague, with drum, ancient,
and soldiers."

Shakespeare's 1 *Henry VI*.   "Enter Talbot, Bedford, and Burgundy,
with scaling ladders: their drums beating a Dead
March."

This is for the scene of the night attack on Orleans, by
which Talbot wins the city.

2 *Henry VI*.   "Drum.   Enter Cade...with infinite numbers."

Ibid.   "Enter Yorke, and his army of Irish, with Drum and Colours."

3 *Henry VI*.   "Enter Oxford, with Drum and Colours."
"Enter Mountague, with Drum and Colours."
"Enter Somerset, with Drum and Colours."
"Enter Clarence, with Drum and Colours."

Here it seems as if no fewer than four drummers were on
the stage together, though it is quite likely that, after

leading in one army, the drummer went back to the door and led in the next.

Richard II. "Enter with Drum and Colours, Bullingbrooke, Yorke," &c.

King Lear (Act IV. Sc. 3). "Enter with Drum and Colours, Cordelia, Gentlemen, and soldiers."

And in the same play, the four armies which appear on the stage in Act V are similarly provided.

In 3 *Henry VI* there are several directions for the entrance of stage-armies prefixed by the order "March," *e.g.*

"A March. Enter Edward, Richard, and their power."
"March. Enter Warwick, Marquess Mountacute, and their army."
"March. Enter Edward, Warwick, &c. and soldiers."

From one of these stage-directions, *viz.*

"March. Enter Mountgomerie, with drum and soldiers,"

and the context, it is plain that these marches were played upon drums only. In Act IV. Sc. 7, Montgomery is represented as arriving with his vassals to help Edward IV. Edward is in doubt concerning the advisability of taking so bold a step as to claim the crown. He thanks Montgomery, but adds that he only claims his dukedom. Montgomery replies—

> "Then fare you well, for I will hence again,
> I came to serve a king, and not a duke:
> Drummer strike up, and let us march away."

This direction then follows:

> "The drum begins to march."

Edward stays him, and consents to be proclaimed king.

The drum was the traditional military instrument of music in England. The national march played upon it, "so famous in all honourable Atchievements and glorious

Warres of this our Kingedome in foraigne parts," was
recorded in a warrant issued by Charles I, ca. 1632[1].
Hence its appearance on the stage in historical plays was
designed to give verisimilitude.   Other stage-directions
where a march is clearly indicated are to be found in the
following plays :

1 *Tamburlaine* (Act II. Sc. 2).   Meander gives the order to his
          drummers, "Strike up the drum and march courageously!"
          and his army moves off, " drums sounding."

Edward III (Act III. Sc. 3).   "Drums.   Enter King Edward, marching ;
          Derby, &c. and forces, and Gobin de Grey."

Drums appear to have come upon the stage sometimes
for duels.   In 2 *Henry VI*, where Peter fights the Armourer, a drummer precedes each as they enter to fight
(Act II. Sc. 3).

Directions for the entrance of Drums and Trumpets on
the stage are not so common.   They seem to have been used
exceptionally for important persons in the historical plays of
Shakespeare's first period.   The following are worthy of note :

Greene's *Orlando Furioso*.   "Enter the Twelve Peers of France, with
          Drum and Trumpets."

Shakespeare's 3 *Henry VI*.   "Flourish.   Enter the King, the Queen,
          Clifford, Northumberland and Young Prince, with Drum
          and Trumpets."

This occurs in the scene at York (Act II. Sc. 2), and it is
worth recording that the earlier quarto *The True Tragedy
of Richard, Duke of York* has " with drum and soldiers "
for the similar direction.   Shakespeare dignified Henry VI
with trumpets, and he does the like for Warwick in the
scene where King Edward is degraded :

"The Drum playing, and Trumpet sounding.   Enter Warwick,
Somerset, and the rest, bringing the King out in his gown, sitting
in a chair."   (3 *Henry VI*, Act IV. Sc. 3.)

[1] Hawkins' *History of Music*, p. 229.

There is one instance of an army moving off the stage led by the sound of drums and trumpets. The last line but one of *The First Part of the Contention, &c.* and 2 *Henry VI*:

"Sound Drum and Trumpets, and to London all,"

implies that the army of the victors at St Albans left the platform headed by martial music, though there is no stage-direction in the texts to prove this.

It was Marlowe who popularised trumpets in battle scenes and "the stately tent of war." His fellow "rhyming mother-wits" used alarums (*i.e.* drum-rolls) to show that a battle was in progress. Marlowe bettered their instruction and directed trumpets to sound "within" for Tamburlaine's battles with Mycetes and Bajazeth. Other playwrights had been content with drums and ensigns for the entrance of their armies. Marlowe added trumpets. For instance:

2 *Tamburlaine* (Act I. Sc. I). "Enter Sigismund," &c. "with drums and trumpets."

Ibid. (Act I. Sc. 3). "Enter Tamburlaine," &c. "with drums and trumpets."

"Enter Theridamas," &c. "with drums and trumpets."

And it may be that, when this innovation was adopted by Greene and Shakespeare[1], he again strove to outdo them. In *Edward II*, he headed his armies with drums and fifes, *e.g.*

"Enter King Edward," &c. "and soldiers with drums and fifes." (Act III. Sc. 2.)

This added pomp and circumstance of war seems to have maintained itself on the Jacobean stage, for in *Lady Alimony* (1633?) an army marches over the platform "with trumpets, fifes, drums, and colours" (Act III. Sc. 2); but the fifes are omitted when the army makes a victorious reappearance in Act V. Sc. 1[2].

---

[1] See above, references to *Orlando Furioso*, and 3 *Henry VI*.

[2] Dodsley-Hazlitt collection, Vol. XIV.

Peaceful processions were accompanied by peaceful music. In Field's *A Woman is a Weathercock* (ca. 1612), Mistress Worldly's wedding procession is headed by waits playing[1] who "walk gravely afore all softly on." It was a custom in grand houses for processions to the banqueting table to be preceded by waits (*i.e.* hautboys). In *The Witches of Lancashire*[2], musicians enter and play before a train of dish-bearers to a banquet.

Music played also whilst funeral processions entered or crossed the platform, but instances are so rare that no rule can be deduced. The following directions for funeral processions all indicate different kinds of music:

2 *Tamburlaine* (Act III. Sc. 2). "Enter Tamburlaine" &c. "four Attendants bearing the hearse of Zenocrate, and the drums sounding a doleful march."

The direction adds "the town burning," which means that, with Marlowe's usual prodigality, red fire was burned.

Titus Andronicus (Act I. Sc. 1). "Sound drums and trumpets. And then enter two of Titus' sons; after them, two men bearing a Coffin covered with black, then two other sons. After them, Titus Andronicus, and then Tamora the Queen of the Goths, and her two sons," &c.

This is for the scene where Titus buries his sons. Trumpets were flourished and sounded when they laid the coffins in the tomb. Probably the inner chamber represented the tomb.

Marston, who carefully indicated his musical directions, added further variety to funeral processions. "The still-flutes sound a mournful senet" for a funeral procession in the *First Part of Antonio and Mellida* (Act V. Sc. 1), and "Organ and Recorders play to a single voice" in *Sophonisba*

---

[1] The stage-direction has "W.P." which must stand for "Waits playing." See Dodsley-Hazlitt collection, Vol. XI. p. 34, note.

[2] Cited by V. Albright, *The Shakesperian Stage*, p. 70.

(Act V. Sc. 4), where Massinissa presents the dead body of Sophonisba to Scipio. The two latter more ambitious musical directions refer to the music of a private theatre. Probably the usual custom in the public theatres was to play dead-marches on drums alone, as in the instance from *Tamburlaine* given above. The dead-marches indicated at the end of the tragedies *Hamlet*, *King Lear*, and *Coriolanus* would be played on the drums alone.

On the platform also in Shakespeare's plays, masquers were often accompanied by musicians. Thus in *Love's Labour's Lost* (Act V. Sc. 2) " Black Moores with musicke " lead in the disguising arranged by the King of Navarre and his friends for the entertainment of the French Princess. In *Much Ado* (Act II) " Maskers with a drum " attend the revels of Leonato's guests. In an entertainment at the house of Timon of Athens, a masque of ladies dressed as Amazons, playing lutes, enters and dances with Timon's guests (Act I. Sc. 2). Sometimes, though not always, musicians came on the platform to play accompaniments to serenades. Cassio enters " with Musitians " to serenade Othello (Act III. Sc. 1). Cloten has made an appointment with a band of musicians when he arrives to serenade Imogen (*Cymbeline*, Act II. Sc. 3). They arrive after him, and come out on the stage to him to play the accompaniment for " Hark! Hark! the lark."

To turn now to examine directions for music off the stage. A frequent musical stage-direction in Elizabethan drama is " Music Within." It seems to denote that unseen musicians played at the side of the platform in the music-room ; or, in playhouses which had no music-room, in its equivalent, the tiring-house on the balcony. The following are examples from early plays. By taking later plays into account a huge list might be compiled.

Greene's *James IV* begins, " Music playing within.   Enter Aster
    Oberon, King of Fairies," &c.

Selimus.   Bajazet retires to the inner chamber.   His nobles " stand
    aside while the curtains are drawn."   Then he speaks.
    " Eunuchs, play me some music while I sleep," and the
    direction " Music within " follows.

Lust's Dominion begins, " Enter Zarack, Balthasar, two Moors taking
    tobacco ; Music sounding within."

Lodge and Greene's *A Looking Glass for London and England.*
    Remilia retires into the inner chamber.   " They draw
    the curtains, and music plays."

It is not clear from this direction whether the musicians
were in the music-room, or within the traverse on the level
of the stage.   Probably the musicians were in the music-
room.   It is difficult to believe that they played within the
inner-chamber in semi-darkness unless they played without
written music or used artificial light.   But in Marston's
Sophonisba (Act IV. Sc. 1), a direction occurs :

    "A treble viol, a base lute, &c., play softly within the canopy[1],"

which implies that musicians were sent into the " cave "
sometimes.

    Songs were often indicated to be sung "within."   There
is a humorous instance in *Albumazar* (1614) by John Tom-
kins.   A cheat tries to sell an old gull a magic ear-trumpet.
He has placed musicians "within."   They play, and then a
song is sung.   The cheat tells the old man that really the
music is being performed at the royal court.   Naturally the
old man is eager to buy this wonderful "autocousticon,"
and pays out ten crowns as earnest money ; but the cheat
avoids detection by telling him that "As yet, the epiglottis
is unperfect" (Act I. Sc. 3).   Further instances of songs

---

[1] Marston appears to have been fond of the combination treble viol and
lute.   It is directed again before Act v.   The effect would be rather like
violin and harp.

"within" are to be found in Marston's *Malcontent* (Act II. Sc. 3), and in Middleton's *Chaste Maid in Cheapside*, where, for the funeral scene (Act V. Sc. 4), "a sad song in the music-room" is directed.

Horns were winded "within" to suggest a hunting scene off the stage, *e.g. Thierry and Theodoret* (Act II. Sc. 2), also *Two Noble Kinsmen* (Act III. Sc. 6) and *King Lear* (Act I. Sc. 4).

Trumpets were sometimes directed to be played "within" when the arrival of a person was indicated. For example:

Selimus. "Sound within. A messenger enters."

Edward III (Act II. Sc. 2). "Trumpet within" followed by "Enter King Edward."

Drums were very often indicated to be played "within" in historical plays. They suggest a distant battle, or the arrival of an army, *e.g.*

Selimus. "Alarum within. Enter Bajazet," &c. "and the Janissaries, at one door; Selimus," &c. "and their soldiers at another."

First Part of the Contention. "Alarmes within...like as it were a fight at sea."

Edward III (Act III. Sc. 1). "Drum within" followed by "Enter King of Bohemia and forces," &c.

A common direction in martial plays is "drum afar off." It is likely that for this drummers played their drums just within the stage-doors. They would most likely stand there because they were often needed to go on the platform with armies. The following directions from Fletcher's *Bonduca* substantiate this.

Bonduca. "Drum softly within, then enter Soldiers with drum and colours." (Act II. Sc. 1.)

Ibid. "Drums within at one place afar off."
"Drums in another place afar off." (Act III. Sc. 3.)

The former implies that the drummer played his drum softly within one of the stage-doors, and then entered with the soldiers. The latter seems to indicate that the positions of the Roman and British armies were suggested by drums played behind alternate sides of the platform.

The following directions are taken from Shakespeare :

3 Henry VI (Act I. Sc. 2). "A march afar off." Edward says at once "I hear their drums."

Richard III (Act V. Sc. 3). "Drum afar off."

Hamlet (Act V. Sc. 2). "March afar off and shout within." Horatio says "Why does the drum come hither," and straightway Fortinbras enters "with Drum, Colours, and Attendants."

Coriolanus (Act I. Sc. 4). "Drums afar off."

In the last stage-direction, the drums were supposed to be within Corioli rousing the Volscians, and they beat during the Roman attack. The whole back-stage represented Corioli. The balcony was "the walls" upon which the Volscians came to parley with the Romans. A side-door represented "the gates." Through it the Volscians made a sortie and drove back the Romans. Through it again Marcius drives them back and is shut in with them.

The meaning of all the foregoing directions containing mention of armies with drums, colours, fifes, and trumpets, is of course that contemporary armies were provided with colours or ensigns, and marched to the thump and rattle of drums. It would appear that fifes date from Elizabethan days their period of employment in the English army[1]. They are supposed to have been adopted in the French

---

[1] Rev. F. W. Galpin, in his *Old English Instruments of Music*, cites an old sketch (Brit. Mus. Aug. A iii) showing an English army ca. 1540 taking the field. Each squadron is headed by a drum and a fife. He gives the size of a military drum which has survived from the reign of Queen Elizabeth as two feet in depth and two feet in diameter.

army from the Swiss after the battle of Marignano (1515), and to have passed from France into the English army.

Above the platform, in front of the players' tiring-house, the balcony was used as a part of the scene in many an old play; and some playwrights, but especially Beaumont and Fletcher, were fond of arranging for songs on the balcony. The following instances are not exhaustive:

Knight of the Burning Pestle. In Act III. Sc. 5, the balcony represents Merrythought's house. Mrs Merrythought returns home and finds "music within." Her husband has invited fiddlers into the house. He comes out on the balcony and sings a laughing song and ballad snatches. Then he calls for more wine and "light music":

> "Play me a light lavolta. Come, be frolic."

Monsieur Thomas. Mary and her maid appear "above." The maid sings:

> "Come up to my window, love." (Act III. Sc. 3.)

The Captain. In Act II. Sc. 2, Frederick and Fabritio, standing on the platform which represents a street, hear a "Lute within":

> "*Fabritio.* Whence is this music?
> *Frederick.* From my sister's chamber."

As they listen to the music, Frank and Clora appear above on the balcony (which represents a house-window) and sing. They look beneath, and Frank exclaims:

> "Clora! come hither! who are these below there?"

From this, it is clear that, for this scene, the musicians sang from the balcony, and the lute accompanied them from within the tiring-house.

In historical plays, the balcony, as we have seen in the example quoted from *Coriolanus*, often represented city walls. Trumpeters were sent up to the balcony to act as heralds, as the following directions show :

Peele's *Edward I.* "Then make the proclamation upon the walls. Sound Trumpets."

Shakespeare's *King John.* "Trumpet sounds. Enter a citizen upon the walls."

Marlowe's fondness for the brazen din of trumpets has already been alluded to. Another peculiar use remains to be mentioned. Besides the directions for battles in 1 *Tamburlaine*, namely, "Trumpets within sound to the battle" (Act II. Sc. 4), and "They sound to the battle within," which occurs twice in Act III. Sc. 3, where other dramatists would have employed drum-alarums, he used "trumpets, within" for coronation scenes. The trumpeters must have been at the back of the stage. Examples are:

1 *Tamburlaine* (Act I. Sc. 1). "Trumpet within," whereupon the Persian lords enter and crown Cosroe. Then trumpeters come out on the platform and are directed to "Sound up the trumpets."

Edward II. "Trumpets within" is directed as Edward III comes on the platform to be crowned. The trumpeters then came out on the platform, for the direction "Trumpets" is given.

Was Marlowe's object to add splendour to his scenes by the contrast of the sound of trumpets muted by being played in a small wooden chamber "within," and their loud clangour when played under the sounding-board in face of the audience ?

Robert Greene perhaps imitated this effect in his *Alphonsus, King of Arragon.* In Act II, Belinus crowns Alphonsus to the sound of "Trumpets and drums sounded within"; but for the crowning of Laelius, King of Naples, by Alphonsus, in Act III, trumpets and drums are sounded on the platform.

There remains yet another curious musical direction to record. Plutarch in his life of Antony records an omen that happened on the eve of Antony's overthrow,—the sound of music was heard and the cries of Bacchantes. To get this supernatural effect, Shakespeare introduced musicians underneath the stage in *Antony and Cleopatra* (Act IV Sc. 3). The direction reads "Music of the Hoboyes is under the stage." Antony's soldiers are filled with foreboding and believe that his familiar spirit is forsaking him. Shakespeare was not original in sending musicians beneath the stage; for two years before, Marston in his *Sophonisba* (1606), played at *Blackfriars*, had done the same thing. In that play he makes the direction "Infernal music plays softly" whilst Syphàx consults the witch Erictho (Act IV. Sc. 1). Surely Marston had seen *Hamlet* and remembered the subterranean "Swear!" (Act I. Sc. 5).

CHAPTER III

MUSICAL INSTRUMENTS AND THEIR USES

Drums — Bells — Trumpets — Sennet — Tucket — Cannon shots — "Alarum"—Horns—Cornets—Hautboys—Recorders—Tabor and Pipe—Viols and Lutes—Lute strings—Organs—Still-pipes—Orchestral music.

BEFORE we attempt to describe the part music took in an Elizabethan play, it is necessary to say something about the musical instruments. They may be classified as follows :

Percussion. Drums, Timbrels, and Bells.

Brass instruments. Sackbuts, Trumpets, and Horns.

Wood instruments. Cornets, Hautboys, Recorders, and Fifes.

Viols. Treble-viols, Viols da gamba, Bass-viols.

Lutes. Treble-lutes, Citterns, Pandores, Bass-lutes.

Drums were of two kinds. The big drum or tabourine[1] was used for playing military marches and national marches (such as that indicated by the direction "Danish march" in *Hamlet*, where the court enters to see the play), or funeral marches[2] (like that at the close of *King Lear*,

---

[1] Shakespeare never calls drums "tabourines" in his stage-directions; but twice in the text of his plays drums are alluded to in poetic diction as tabourines, and are called upon together with trumpets to sound for an exit in state. E.g. *Troilus and Cressida* (Act IV. Sc. 5, near the end), and *Antony and Cleopatra* (Act IV. Sc. 8, end).

[2] In *The Spanish Tragedy*, a dead-march was played by trumpets (see Act IV. Sc. 4).

"Exeunt with a dead march"). Small drums called timbrels were hoops of wood covered with parchment only on one side. They were probably used in masquers' processions and in plays dealing with the East. They were employed at *The Rose* theatre, but there are no stage-directions indicating their use[1].

It was on the drum or tabourine that the drummers played their "alarums," that is to say drum-rolls to indicate that a battle was being fought, and also "retreats." They were employed on the stage, and also behind the scenes if it was desired to imitate a distant battle. Directions for alarums are so numerous in historical plays that it is not necessary to give instances. They can be found by dozens in Shakespeare's Histories, even in the First Folio; and later editors have inserted them in great profusion.

The "alarum" was properly the military signal to battle. For example in *Henry V* (Act II), at the siege of Harfleur before King Henry's famous oration—

> "Once more unto the breach, dear friends, once more;
> Or close the wall up with our English dead:"

the stage-direction runs: "Alarum. Scaling ladders at Harflew." "Alarums and Excursions" meant skirmishes of opposing forces rallied by drums. Drums were used to rally as well as to sound to the attack, and "alarums" is used indiscriminately for attacking and rallying signals. For example, in *Edward III* the direction occurs (Act III. Sc. 4): "Alarums, as of a battle joined. Enter a many Frenchmen, flying; Prince, and English, pursuing; and exeunt"—so that evidently the drums beat not only before, but during the fight.

---

[1] Cf. Henslowe's inventory at *The Rose* including one drum and three timbrels. There is just a possibility that these "timbrels" were kettledrums used for sounding alarums. If so, *timbrel* was confused with the French *timbale*.

Bells appear to have been introduced by Marlowe. In his *Jew of Malta* (1588) he directs "Bells within" (Act IV. Sc. 1), and makes Barabas say: "How sweet the bells ring now the nuns are dead." Doubtless bells were used for the directions: "The clock strikes eleven," "the clock strikes the half hour," "the clock strikes twelve" in *Doctor Faustus* (Act V. Sc. 4). After midnight has struck, devils enter and bear Faustus off to hell[1]. Other theatres adopted bells. In *Macbeth*, a bell is the signal for Duncan's assassination (Act II. Sc. 1):

> "*Macbeth.* Go bid thy mistress, when my drink is ready,
> She strike upon the bell."

It is the bell again that rouses the castle when the deed is accomplished. One imagines that Shakespeare would have bells for the wedding in *Much Ado*, and for the graveyard scene in *Hamlet*, though there are no directions in the texts. Henslowe's inventory shows that he had bells at *The Rose* playhouse.

A sackbut, notwithstanding its biblical name, was simply the deep-toned brass instrument now known as the trombone. Sackbuts were used sometimes for the conventional three blasts before the entrance of the "prologue," but from the few references to them it seems as if they were not in common use in theatres. They were, however, part of the household music at the royal court.

Trumpets were of two shapes, a long open tuba shaped like our coach-horns, or a bent military bugle larger than our modern bugles. Neither kind was fitted with keys. That was a later invention. Hence, unlike sackbuts, which

---

[1] There is an imitation of this scene in the Induction to *The Merry Devil of Edmonton*. "The chime goes, in which time Fabell is oft seen to stare about him, and hold up his hands." When the bell ceases, Coreb, Fabell's familiar spirit, enters to carry him off to hell.

Plate IV

Drums and Trumpets

1 and 2. *Trumpets*   3. *Drum*   4. *Tabourine*

could play a complete chromatic scale, trumpets could only play the notes we are accustomed to hear in fanfares and bugle calls. The series in the scale of C would be

There is such an abundance of directions for flourishes and sounding of trumpets that it is impossible to begin to quote. Over fifty may be found in the First Folio edition of Shakespeare's plays alone. Let it suffice to say that all the courtly and warlike etiquette of trumpets was carried out in the public theatres. Trumpets were "flourished" for the entry of kings, generals, tribunes, and players; or for their exits. Sometimes also they were flourished before the Prologue and after the Epilogue[1]. They were "sounded" for greetings, proclamations, processions, betrothals, reconciliations, coronations, parleys, challenges and tournaments[2]. The usual stage-directions are "Flourish," "Trumpets," "Sound," and they all indicate short fanfares on the open notes, such as trumpeters still play on ceremonial occasions.

Two less obvious directions are found. A Sennet appears to have been a prelude played upon trumpets. It was more elaborate and lasted longer than a "flourish." The word is usually derived from Lat. *sonare*. Probably it is a doublet of "sonnet" from Ital. *sonetto*. A sennet is

---

[1] E.g. *The Two Noble Kinsmen* (Q. 1634), as played at *Blackfriars* "with great applause."

[2] Professor R. H. Case has pointed out to me that trumpets were also sounded during ceremonial drinking. He instances the line "Make battery to our ears with the loud music," *Antony and Cleopatra* (Act II. Sc. 7); also Beaumont and Fletcher's *Scornful Lady* (Act I. Sc. 1, beginning); Davenant's *Albovine* (Act II); Shadwell's *Miser* (Act III. Sc. 2, and Act IV. Sc. 1); *Hamlet* (Act I. Sc. 2, l. 125, Act I. Sc. 4, Act V. Sc. 2).

always directed for the entrance (or exit) in state of a most important personage.   For instance :

First part of Jeronimo begins, " Sound a Signet.   Enter the King of Spain, Duke of Castile," &c.

Shakespeare's 2 *Henry VI.* " Sound a sennet" occurs where the king enters parliament (Act I. Sc. 3).

Henry VIII. " Trumpets, Sennet, and Cornets," are indicated during the procession to the Consistory (Act II. Sc. 4).

Probably this direction means a sennet played by both trumpets and cornets.

King Lear. A sennet sounds in the first scene, where Lear enters with his court to divide the kingdom.

Fletcher's *Valentinian.* " A synnet, with trumpets" is directed (Act V. Sc. 8), where the emperor enters his presence-chamber.

Marlowe's *Doctor Faustus* (Q. 1604). " Sound a Sonnet.   Enter the Pope and the Cardinal of Lorrain to the banquet, with friars attending."

For the same scene, Q. 1616 has:

" A Sennet whilst the banquet is brought in ; and then enter Faustus and Mephistophilis in their own shape."

Ibid. (Q. 1616). " A Sennet.   Enter Charles, the German Emperor," &c.

This scene offers proof that a sennet was played on trumpets.   The Emperor desires to see Alexander the Great.   Faust offers to gratify the Emperor.   He orders his familiar—

> " Mephistophilis, away !
> And with a solemn noise of *trumpets*' sound
> Present before this royal Emperor,
> Great Alexander and his beauteous paramour."

Then comes the following direction—

" Sennet.   Enter at one door the Emperor Alexander, at the other Darius ; they meet, Darius is thrown down, Alexander kills him ; takes off his crown and offering to go out, his paramour meets him, he embraceth her, and sets Darius' crown upon her head ; and coming back, both salute the Emperor, who, leaving his state, offers to embrace them, which, Faustus seeing, suddenly stays him. *Then trumpets cease, and music sounds.*"

It is clear from the latter direction that trumpets played sennets, and also that the sound of trumpets was not designated music. Another fact revealed by this evidence is that a sennet was not a fanfare but a short piece of music. It lasted long enough for a stage-procession to file in, for a banquet to be laid, or for the tournament between Alexander and Darius to take place. The procession to the Consistory court in *Henry VIII* would require about two minutes, and the scene from *Doctor Faustus* where Alexander appears, two minutes at least.

An instance of a sennet directed for an exit occurs in *Henry V* at the end of the last scene, in which the king is betrothed to Katharine of France. The direction reads "Senet. Exeunt," and denotes simply a postlude whilst the French and English courts filed off the stage. It has nothing to do with the betrothal. The actual betrothal was signalised by a "flourish." Similarly in *Coriolanus* (Act II), where the Roman hero is given his name of honour, Coriolanus, the naming is signalised by a "flourish," but the signal for the entrance of Cominius, Titus Lartius, and Coriolanus is "sennet."

Sennet music has disappeared entirely. It was played from memory by musicians who transmitted it to their apprentices as part of their mystery. At the private theatres, sennets were played upon cornets. A sennet on the cornets was often played during a dumb-show.

That the other direction, Tucket, was a trumpet fanfare can be shown from *King Lear*. Twice the direction "Tucket within" is found. After the first, Gloucester says "Hark! the Duke's trumpets" (*K. Lear*, Act II.

Sc. 1). After the second, Cornwall asks "What trumpet's that?" (*Ibid.* Act II. Sc. 2). Similarly in the tournament scene in *Richard II*, Quarto 1 has the direction "The trumpets sound. Enter Duke of Hereford appellant in armour"; but the First Folio reads "Tucket. Enter Hereford and Harold." Tuckets announce the arrival of heralds and messengers, and of courtly persons less exalted in rank than those distinguished with sennets. A curious use occurs in *Timon of Athens.* "Sound Tucket" is directed (Act I. Sc. 2) when the masque of ladies dressed as Amazons enters Timon's banquet[1].

Trumpets and drums together were used for occasions of great pomp, such as Warwick's deposition of King Edward in 3 *Henry VI*, and the coronation of Laelius, King of Naples, in Greene's *Alphonsus, King of Arragon.* They sound when Cominius names Coriolanus for the first time (Act I. Sc. 8); and, a rather curious use, they play for the coming of Titus Andronicus to the tomb of his ancestors to bury his dead sons and to sacrifice the eldest son of Tamora, Queen of the Goths (Act I. Sc. 2). A curious direction is to be found in *Richard III* (Act IV. Sc. 4). "K. Richard marching with Drummes and Trumpets[2]" is intercepted by his mother and Queen Elizabeth. As they begin to curse him for his villainies he calls out—

> "A flourish trumpets, strike alarum drums:
> Let not the Heavens hear these tell-tale women
> Rail on the Lord's anointed. Strike, I say."

—and the din of drums and trumpets drowns their reproaches.

---

[1] Francis Markham's *Five Decades of Epistles of Warre* (London, 1622) mentions "tucquet" as the cavalry signal to march (Decade 3, Epistle 1). Cited in article "Military Sounds and Signals," Grove's *Dictionary of Music*, Vol. III.

[2] Quarto 1597.

A similar direction is indicated in *Edward III* (Act v. Sc. 1), where the six burghers of Calais enter in their shirts and with halters about their necks to surrender the town. They appeal to Edward III for mercy, and he replies :

> "Contemptuous villains ! call ye now for truce?
> Mine ears are stopp'd against your bootless cries.
> Sound drums [*Alarum*]"—

and the noise of drums drowns their appeal. They persist in their endeavour to make peace, and owing to the intercession of Queen Philippa their efforts meet with success.

It is likely that this incident was an imitation of the above scene in *Richard III*. *Edward III* followed this play on the stage. There is no mention of the entreaties of the burghers being drowned by the noise of drums in either Froissart or Holinshed, so that probably the incident was introduced by the dramatist owing to the success of the similar scene in *Richard III*.

Another quaint musical effect was the combination of trumpet blasts and cannon shots. For instance, "Sound trumpets and a peal of ordnance" (*First Part of Jeronimo*). "Trumpets sound, and chambers are discharged within" (*Battle of Alcazar*, Act III. Sc. 4). "Trumpets sound, and a shot goes off" when the king drinks wassail in *Hamlet* (Act V) during the fencing match. A mischance in carrying out this stage-direction during a performance of *All is True*, or *Henry VIII*, caused the destruction of the first *Globe* theatre on June 29th, 1613. "King Henry, making a mask at the Cardinal Wolsey's house, and certain cannons being shot off at his entry, some of the paper or other stuff wherewith one of them was stopped did light on the thatch, where, being thought at first but an idle smoke, and their eyes more attentive to the show, it kindled inwardly and ran round like a train, consuming within less than an hour the whole house to the very grounds[1]."

It remains to point out some exceptional uses of trumpets. We have said that marches were played by drums alone. This was the custom of the time. Nevertheless *The Spanish Tragedy* concludes with the direction, " The trumpets sound a dead march" (Act IV. Sc. 4). We have also said that "alarums" were played on big drums called tabourines. This is true as a general rule, but there are one or two exceptions in the text of Shakespeare's plays. All occur in tournament scenes where trumpets sound to the attack[2]. In one in *2 Henry VI*, before the fight of Peter with the Armourer, York says (Act II. Sc. 3):

" Sound, trumpets, alarum to the combatants."

No stage-direction follows. Modern composite texts of Shakespeare have a stage-direction " Alarum " at this point, but it is an interpolation. It does not occur in the First Folio.

Another instance is to be found in *Troilus and Cressida* (Act IV. Sc. 5). A direction "Alarum" occurs, then Hector and Ajax fight, and shortly after " Trumpets cease " occurs. " Alarum " here seems definitely to be associated with the sound of trumpets. Yet another instance occurs in *King Lear* (Act V. Sc. 3). At the beginning of the duel between Edgar and the Bastard, the latter ends his flyting with the words " Trumpets speak !"; and immediately the direction " Alarums " occurs, and the duel begins.

---

[1] Reliq. Wotton., edit. 1672, p. 425.   Cited Collier, *Annals*, Vol. III. pp. 298, 299.

[2] On a miserere seat in Worcester Cathedral is a carving of a tournament between two knights. At the right side of the picture a page is blowing a clarion. On the left, a laughing serving-man is playing an alarum on the kettledrums. See Rev. F. W. Galpin's *Old English Instruments of Music*, Pl. 49.

It is to this use of trumpets in tournaments that Warwick refers when challenging Clifford in the fifth act of 2 *Henry VI*—

> "Now when the angry trumpet sounds alarum,
> And dead men's cries do fill the empty air,
> Clifford I say, come forth and fight with me";

or, as the *First Part of the Contention*, &c., has it,

> "Now whilst the angry Trumpets sound alarmes."

These instances give the word "alarum" a wider significance than it usually gets. The fact that trumpets sound alarums for duels and tournaments shows that as its derivation implies (Italian *all' arme*) the word meant a signal to battle, but although on the stage this was oftenest given by drums, drums were not the essential feature.

Horns were required in some Elizabethan plays, and the kind used seems to have been a conical brass tube so bent that it could almost encircle a man's neck. It could produce the same notes as the trumpet[1]. In Shakespeare's time, horns were not used in combination with other instruments. They were simply hunting instruments. On them were played "peals" corresponding to the "flourishes" of trumpets, and a punctilious etiquette fixed the correct set of notes for each operation of the chase. It was

---

[1] Modern orchestral horns, which are a development of this instrument, produce a softer tone than trumpets partly because their mouthpiece is funnel-shaped $\bigvee$, whereas trumpets have a cup-shaped mouthpiece $\bigvee$. Rev. F. W. Galpin says: "The recognised distinction between the Horn and the Trumpet is found in the shape of the tube. Instruments of the Trumpet type have for the greater part of their length a tube of cylindrica bore opening outwards towards the end into a broader bell.......The Horn type includes those instruments in which the tube tapers gradually from mouthpiece to bell, and it is represented by the Bugle, Hunting horns (great and small) and the two classes of Cornets ancient and modern." *Old English Instruments of Music*, p. 182.

considered a manly accomplishment to play the hunting horn.

> "The horn, the horn, the lusty horn
> Is not a thing to laugh to scorn."

Every gentleman who kept hounds could wind it, so that when Talbot "winds his horn" to call his men into the Countess of Auvergne's castle (1 *Henry VI*, Act II. Sc. 3), it was not at all an unnatural pre-arranged signal.

Hunting "peals" were introduced for the hunting scenes in *Titus Andronicus* (Act II), *The Two Noble Kinsmen* (Act III. Scs. 5 and 6), *Thierry and Theodoret* (Act II. Sc. 2), and in Thomas Heywood's play *A Woman Killed with Kindness* (Act I. Sc. 3). They awakened Lysander and Demetrius from their sleep in the wood (*Midsummer Night's Dream*, Act IV), and they were used in *King Lear* (Act I. Sc. 4) to indicate that Lear is returning from the chase. In Nash's *Will Summer's Last Will and Testament*[1] the direction " Enter Orion like a hunter, with a horn about his neck" occurs, and we must not forget that it was with a post-horn that Truewit roused old Morose in Jonson's *Silent Woman* (Act II. Sc. 1).

The cornet was a kind of horn made of a hollowed tusk, or of wood covered with leather, with a mouthpiece like the cup of a trumpet. It was bored with six holes in front, covered by the fingers, and one hole on the reverse side, covered by a thumb. Its compass was a chromatic scale of slightly over two octaves. The cornet has fallen into complete disuse. It was quite distinct from the modern cornet[2]. Cornets were played in sets of three, with a sackbut for the bass. The treble cornet had a compass

[1] Dodsley Hazlitt collection, Vol. VIII.

[2] An excellent account is to be found in Rev. F. W. Galpin's *Old English Instruments of Music*. See also article "Zincke" in Grove's *Dictionary of Music*.

of about two octaves from middle D, the alto was tuned a fifth, and the tenor cornet an octave lower. The tenor cornet was bent in shape something like the letter **S**. The cornet was fingered like a hautboy, but it produced a reedy trumpet-like tone. The cornet stop on the organ was originally a copy of it.

Cornets were used in the private theatres where the noisy din of brazen trumpets would have been unbearable. There they fulfilled all the uses of trumpets at public theatres, as the following typical directions will show:

Marston's 1 *Antonio and Mellida*[1]. "The cornets sound a battle within."

Ibid. "The cornets sound a flourish"—for a greeting.

Ibid. "The cornets sound a senet"—for an entry (Act I. Sc. 1).

Ibid. "The cornets sound a senet, and the Duke goes out in state" (Act II. Sc. 1).

Marston's 2 *Antonio and Mellida.* Act II is preceded by a dumb-show. The direction begins "The cornets sound a senet," and ends "Cornets cease, and he speaks."

The Two Noble Kinsmen[2]. "Cornets, trumpets, sound as to a charge"—for the Tournament "within" (Act V. Sc. 3).

Ibid. "Cornets in sundry places"—to indicate "people a Maying" (Act III. Sc. 1).

As the cornets formed a complete band, they played between the acts at *Blackfriars*. Marston has frequent mention of them in his plays. His usual direction is "The cornets sound for the Act." Sometimes the organ accompanied them. At the end of the first act of *Sophonisba* "cornets and organs" played "loud full music for the Act." They also accompanied voices, either singly, as in *The Malcontent* (Act V. Sc. 3), "Cornets: the song to the cornets, which playing the mask enters"; or with the organ, as in

---

[1] "Played by the Children of Paules," ca. 1602, see title-page of the play.

[2] "Presented at the Blackfriers by the Kings Maiesties servants."

Sophonisba (Act I. Sc. 2), "Chorus, with cornets, organs and voices." And they played dance music, as in *The Malcontent*, where "The cornets sound the measure" (Act V. Sc. 3). A curious use is before the prologue to *Sophonisba*. Overtures were not played in Elizabethan theatres, but here the cornets played a march as a sort of prelude as the prologue speaker and his attendants enter and retire. The direction reads "Cornets sounding a march, enter the Prologue," and again at the end of his speech "Cornets sound a march."

Cornets were not in regular use at public theatres, but cornet players were engaged there for certain plays. For example, cornets were used in the scene of the trial of Queen Katherine in *Henry VIII* (Act I. Sc. 2). In *Coriolanus*, cornets are used to distinguish Tullus Aufidius and his Volscians from the Romans (cf. Act I. Sc. 10 with the previous scenes); for the Romans have drums and trumpets in the field, though they are given cornets in the senate (Act III. Sc. 1). Cornets were employed in *The Merchant of Venice* for the casket scenes. They play "flourishes" for the entrance and exit of all the suitors (Act II) except Bassanio, who being the favoured wooer is given the best music the house can provide (Act III. Sc. 2).

Hautboys, the original of modern orchestral oboes, were conical wooden tubes with six holes in front for the fingers and a thumb-hole behind. The sound was produced by the vibrations of a double reed. Their popular names were "shawms" and "waits." The former shows their kinship to the reedy pipe of the Arcadian shepherd (O. Fr. *chalemel*; L. *calamus*). The latter indicates that they were a favourite instrument of the watchmen. A treble hautboy was practically the same thing as a musette or shepherd's pipe, and yet its case, said Sir John Falstaff,

Plate V

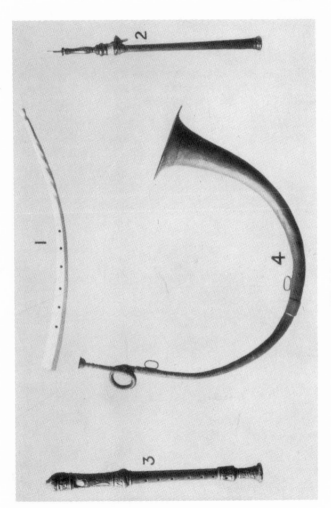

Wind Instruments

1. *Cornet*   2. *Hautboy*   3. *Recorder*   4. *Horn*

was a "mansion" for Justice Shallow. Hautboys were played in "consorts," usually of four different sizes, and the players as well as the instruments were called "waits." The tenor hautboy developed into the cor-anglais, and the bass of the consort of hautboys is now the bassoon.

Consorts of hautboys were the music prescribed by etiquette for banquets. An old engraving in the chateau at Fontainebleau entitled " Le festin du roy " shows hautboys big and little playing for a court entertainment. This was their chief employment in Elizabethan theatres. For the banquet scene in *The Maid's Tragedy* (Act IV. Sc. 2) " Hautboys play within." At Timon of Athens' first banquet " Hoboyes playing loud music " are directed ; and when the guests fall to dancing, it is to " a lofty strain or two to the Hoboyes." " Hoboyes and torches " conduct Duncan to Dunsinane (*Macbeth*, Act I. Sc. 6), and later (Sc. 7) the hautboys play as the servants carry in the dishes for supper. Hautboys, again, play for Wolsey's entertainment (*Henry VIII*, Act I. Sc. 4).

One special use of hautboys deserves to be mentioned. When Coriolanus and his Volscians depart from Rome (*Coriolanus*, Act V. Sc. 4) the Romans express their joy with music.

> " The trumpets, sackbuts, psalteries, and fifes,
> Tabors, and cymbals, and the shouting Romans
> Make the sun dance."

To get the loudest musical effect the theatre could provide, the stage-direction provides :

> " Trumpets, Hoboyes, Drums beate, altogether."

The tone of hautboys was shrill and reedy. They never accompanied voices in the theatre. Bacon observes in *Sylva Sylvarum* (1627): " the voice and pipes alone, agree not so well " (Cent. III. Par. 278).

The recorder was a vertical flute with a whistle mouth-piece. It had usually seven finger-holes, and one hole for the thumb at the back. It was commonly played in sets of four or six, and a consort played music in three parts—treble, tenor, and bass. The recorder was not fingered like the flageolet. The latter had only four finger-holes in front, and two thumb-holes behind[1].

The tone of a recorder was sweet and flute-like. As Bacon remarks in his *Sylva Sylvarum*: "the Recorder and Stringed Musick agree well" (Cent. III. Par. 278). Its soft mournful tone often accompanied a consort of strings, when it commonly played the alto part. Recorders were not in common use in the theatres, though they seem to have been used occasionally at *Blackfriars* theatre to provide solemn music. In *The Two Noble Kinsmen*, where Emilia offers incense to Diana (Act V. Sc. 1), "Still music of records" is prescribed. In Marston's *Sophonisba*, "organ and recorders play to a single voice," where Massinissa presents Sophonisba's dead body to Scipio (Act V. Sc. 4). In Fletcher's *Bonduca* (Act III. Sc. 1), the British queen leaves the druids' temple, "recorders playing[2]." Recorders were also in use occasionally at the court performances. Nash's court comedy *Will Summer's Last Will and Testament* (? 1592) has the direction "Enter Solstitium...brought in by a number of Shepherds, playing upon recorders."

Flutes were not in use in the heyday of Elizabethan drama. They are mentioned amongst the instruments which played for the dumb-shows in the early tragedies *Gorboduc* and *Jocasta*, but afterwards they appear to have

[1] An exhaustive description of the recorder and literary references thereto is to be found in *Six Lectures on the Recorder* by Christopher Welch, M.A. Oxon. 1911.

[2] Milton imagines the army of Hell in *Paradise Lost*, Book I, marching to the "Dorian mood of flutes and soft recorders."

fallen into disuse. A small-sized flute, called a fife, was used by masquers and soldiers. In *The Merchant of Venice*, Shakespeare makes Shylock say to Jessica :

> "What ! are there masques ? Hear you me, Jessica :
> Lock up my doors ; and when you hear the drum
> And the vile squeaking of the wry-neck'd fife,
> Clamber not you up to the casements then."
>
> (Act II. Sc. 5.)

The fife is called "wry-neck'd" because as the player puts his lips to the blow-hole his face is half turned to the left.

The fife and drum together were military instruments. They are brought on the stage in Marlowe's *Edward II*, and in *Lady Alimony*, but never became popular. Shakespeare only once prescribed drum and fife. In *Timon of Athens* (Act IV. Sc. 3)—the scene where Timon finds gold in the wood and gives it away to Phrynia and Timandra, the mistresses of Alcibiades—Timon hears a "March afarre off," that is to say, within one of the side doors, and then Alcibiades enters "with drum and fife in war-like manner, and Phrynia and Timandra." It is difficult to account for this solitary direction. The date of *Timon of Athens*, 1607 or 1608, precludes any imitation of Marlowe's *Edward II*. No fifes are indicated in the other plays. Even in *Coriolanus* (Act V. Sc. 4), where fifes are indicated in the text along with trumpets, sackbuts, psalteries, tabors, and cymbals, only trumpets, hautboys, and drums were played according to the stage-direction.

In I *Henry IV* (Act III. Sc. 3), Prince Hal is preparing to set out on the expedition against Hotspur. Falstaff meets him "playing on his truncheon like a fife," and asks : "Must we all march ?" Needless to say, he is poking fun at the military music of the day. There is also a reference to the fife in the text of *Much Ado About Nothing* (Act II.

Sc. 3). Benedick, speaking of Claudio in love, says:
" I have known when there was no music with him
but the drum and the fife, and now had he rather hear
the tabor and pipe"—meaning that whereas he used
to delight in martial music, now he likes jigs and
merriment.

Tabor and pipe were a tiny drum, and a small flageolet
with three holes. Although the pipe only had three holes,
quite an extensive scale could be played on it by a skilful
performer. The comedians Tarleton and Kempe were
expert players. They commonly gave an entertainment
on the stage wherein they tapped the drum with one hand,
played the pipe with the other, danced jigs with their feet,
and kept up a busy fire of jests and witticism. Tabor and
pipe were used for accompanying morris-dances at rural
merry-makings. Hence Dull's anxiety in *Love's Labour's
Lost* (Act V. Sc. 1) to play them for the Nine Worthies.
Such a stage use is to be found in Dekker's *Shoemaker's
Holiday*. Simon Eyre the shoemaker is made sheriff of
London, and his apprentices come with pipe and tabor to
the Lord Mayor's dinner to entertain the guests with their
morris-dances (Act III. Sc. 5). Shakespeare introduces
tabor and pipe on the stage in *The Tempest* (Act III. Sc. 2),
where Ariel appears with these " instruments of torture" to
torment Stephano and Çaliban.

The stringed instruments in use in Elizabethan theatres
were viols and lutes. The essential difference between
them was that viols were played with a bow, like instruments
of the violin type, whereas lutes were played by plucking
the strings with the right hand like modern guitars. Viols
were the same shape as our orchestral double-bass. They
had usually six strings tuned in thirds and fourths, and
their finger-boards were marked with frets to show the

Plate VI

Stringed Instruments

1. *Viol* 2. *Cithern* 3. *Lute*
4. *Viol da gamba* 5. *Lute with additional harp-strings*

left hand where to stop the required notes[1]. Three sizes were in common use, the treble viol slightly bigger than our violins, the tenor viol bigger than a viola, and the bass viol or viol da gamba, which was played like a 'cello between the knees. Their tone was reedy and penetrating, but not as loud as that of instruments of the violin type. The compass was slightly over two octaves. The lowest open string on the treble viol was the D an octave below middle D, the tenor was a fifth, and the gamba an octave lower. Thus their complete range was about that of the human voice.

Lutes were of various shapes and sizes. The treble lute in common use was shaped like a large mandoline. The number of sets of strings on lutes varied, but the commonest number was six, of which the five lower were attached in pairs, making eleven in all. The single string, or "chanterelle," played the melody, and the doubled strings the accompaniment. Instruments of the guitar type called a cithern and pandore (or bandore)[2] played the alto and tenor parts respectively. They lacked chanterelles and only played a chordal accompaniment. The bass lute (chittarone or archlute) was a large instrument of the lute type, with additional open strings on a second head, so that it was really a combination of harp and lute. It is impossible to speak definitely of either shape or the number

---

[1] The frets on viols and lutes were strings of catgut tied round the finger board. On the pandore and cithern, which were strung with wire, frets were of metal or ivory inlaid. See Rev. F. W. Galpin's *Old English Instruments of Music*, p. 47. A violist or lutanist was supposed to be sufficiently expert to put a new fret on his instrument if the old fret broke loose. Hence Hamlet's "Though you can fret me, you cannot play upon me."

[2] The cithern was shaped like a flat-backed mandoline, with four pairs of wire strings. It was played with a plectrum. The pandore was flat-backed, rather like a guitar, and was strung usually with six pairs of strings.

of strings on Elizabethan lutes. New strings were added, involving new methods of fingering, to accommodate lutes to greater demands put upon them by musical development, until finally they were strung with twenty-four strings. Their finger-boards were fretted like viols. Lute players did not read music from staves like other musicians, but had a peculiar notation of their own called a "tablature[1]."

In the theatres, viols and lutes were used chiefly to accompany songs. There were not quartets of both sorts. The common practice was to have a "broken consort" consisting of a treble and a bass viol, with lute, cithern, and pandore[2]. This is confirmed by the evidence of contemporary music-books such as Morley's *First Booke of Consort Lessons* (1599) and Leighton's *Tears, or Lamentations of a Sorrowful Soul* (1614). The usual stage-directions for the use of viols and lutes are "music" or "soft music," but directions for the entrance of singers and masquers with stringed instruments are quite common.

There is such a mass of directions in which viols and lutes would take part that it is impossible to furnish a catalogue. They would, however, accompany most songs, and many dances. The fiddles "go finely," says the Citizen's wife in the interval after Act I of *The Knight of the Burning Pestle*, and in this gap a boy comes on and dances a jig. Probably they played whilst Bassanio made

[1] In a tablature, a stave of six lines represented the strings. Letters of the alphabet written thereon represented the frets to be pressed, and musical notes to express duration were placed above and below the stave.

[2] A whole consort was a band composed of instruments of one kind, such as a "nest" of cornets, a "chest" of viols, or a "set" of recorders. A broken consort was a small orchestra made up of instruments of various kinds. It might include voices.

his choice (*Merchant of Venice*, Act III. Sc. 2). It was the melody of viols for sure that made a "dying close" when Orsino bade them "play on" (*Twelfth Night*, Act I. Sc. 1). It was viols and lutes in the hands of "Sneak's noise" that provided entertainment for Falstaff and Mistress Doll Tearsheet (2 *Henry IV*, Act II. Sc. 4). And we may assume that when music was played between the acts of a play, the "consort" or band of stringed instruments did most of the work.

The viol da gamba, corresponding to our violoncello, was a fashionable instrument for men[1], and was often hung up as a property when the stage represented an interior. In stage-directions it is commonly called simply "the viol." In Jonson's *Every Man out of his Humour*, done at *The Globe* (1599), Fastidious "takes down the viol and plays" (Act III. Sc. 3). In the same author's *Poetaster*, produced at *Blackfriars* (1601), Crispinus takes down the viol and accompanies his own song (Act IV. Sc. 1). It was such a viol probably that Cerimon bade his servant play to waken Thaisa from her trance (*Pericles*, Act III. Sc. 2). So that evidently several players could play the viol da gamba well enough to play in public[2].

Lutes were very popular in Elizabethan England. Lute-strings were often given as presents, and according to Greene and Lodge in their *Looking Glass for London and England* (1594) they were forced by usurers on their unfortunate victims. In that play, Thrasybulus, who

[1] Aguecheek in *Twelfth Night* "plays o' the viol de gamboys and speaks three or four languages word for word without book."

[2] Cf. also Marston's 2 *Antonio and Mellida* (Act III. Sc. 2). Balurdo enters "with a bass viol" and sings. Also in Middleton's *Roaring Girl* (Act IV. Sc. 1), the heroine dressed as a man picks up the viol and accompanies her song.

borrowed £40, had to take only £10 in money and the rest in lute-strings, which he could only sell for five pounds[1]. Had such an experience happened to one of them? One wonders...

Some of the songs in the plays were accompanied by lutanists alone. For example in Dekker's *Honest Whore,* Bellafront is "discovered sitting with a lute," and sings (Act III. Sc. 3). Marston's *Dutch Courtesan* (1605) contains the directions "Enter Franceschina with her lute." "She sings to her lute" (Act I. Sc. 2). Nor must we forget the part the lute plays in *The Taming of the Shrew.* Hortensio disguises as "a schoolmaster well seen in music" in order to woo the gentle Bianca. Before he can approach to teach her the gamut of love, she keeps him employed for half an hour in tuning his lute; and her sister breaks the lute over his head for saying "she mistook her frets" (Act II. Sc. 1). Owing to their double strings lutes were difficult to keep in tune. This was an excuse for Bianca, and it may have served for the Shrew.

Organs were used in the private theatres, following the custom of the court theatre, where an organ had been in use ever since the days of Moralities and Interludes[2]. Marston indicated that an organ and other instruments played between the acts of his *Sophonisba,* at *Blackfriars.* In Middleton's *A Mad World, My Masters,* played by the "Children of Poules".(1608), a piece of dialogue is introduced simply to show off the organ. Sir Bounteous Progress, a philistine, proud of the amount he has spent

---

[1] Cf. also Will Summer's statement in Nash's *Will Summer's Last Will and Testament*: "I know...another that ran into debt, in the space of four or five year, above fourteen thousand pound in lute-strings and grey paper."

[2] In 1516, Henry VIII paid "To one Sigemonde Skeyf, an Almayn, for an instrument called a Regalle, £22" ("The Kynges boke of payments" in the Chapter House, Westminster, quoted by Collier, *Annals,* Vol. I. p. 76).

on his ornate instrument, is depicted showing a visitor
round his country house.

> " *Sir B.*   Your Lordship ne'er heard my organs?
>   *Follywit.*   Heard of 'em, Sir Bounteous, but never heard 'em.
>   *Sir B.*   They're but double-gilt my lord; some hundred and fifty
>   pound will fit your lordship with such another pair."

Then he calls for music, and "The Organs play" (Act II.
Sc. 1). At *Blackfriars* theatre, to judge from directions in
plays acted there, the organ together with recorders or
even cornets accompanied songs, and along with cornets
often played in the interval between acts. Organs were
not used in the public theatres.

Still-pipes are mentioned in the stage-directions of
some plays which were performed at private theatres.
They played for dumb-shows occasionally in the old
Inns of Court plays. "A sweet noise of still pipes" was
heard before the second act of Wilmot's *Tancred and
Gismunda* (1568). In Gascoigne's *Jocasta* (1566), during
the dumb-show before the fifth act, "the still pipes sounded
a very mournful melodye, in which time there came upon
the stage a woman clothed in a white garment." Mr Galpin
thinks still-pipes were a kind of crooked shawm called
krumhorns or cromornes, the tone of which is preserved
in the organ stop called Cremona[1]. Another explanation
is that they were recorders. The "noise" or harmony of
a consort of shawms could scarcely be described as sweet,
whereas the word sweet aptly describes the tone of recorders. Also in Marston's plays 1 *Antonio and Mellida*
(Act V. Sc. 1), 2 *Antonio and Mellida* (Act IV. Sc. 1), "still-
flutes" are indicated. In the former play they "sound a
mournful senet" for a funeral procession. If these were
the same instrument, still-pipes were almost certainly

[1] *Old English Instruments of Music*, p. 164.

recorders. A shawm could not truly be called a flute, whereas a recorder might be. Also the sweet and sad notes of recorders would provide fitting music for a funeral cortège[1].

It is necessary to guard against the notion that the numerous instruments used in the Elizabethan theatres formed an orchestra. Orchestral music in the modern meaning of the term was quite unknown. The nearest approach thereto was the combination of viols, citherns and pandores, with recorders and flutes. This was called " broken musick or consort musick." Cornets and hautboys were too harsh in tone to agree with stringed music, and separate bands consisting wholly of instruments of either sort were the rule. Trumpets also, although sometimes combined with drums or cornets, or even hautboys, were usually played alone.

Thus whilst there was no attempt to obtain a mass of orchestral sound, there was a real striving for musical " colour," and all sorts of small combinations of instruments are indicated. Dramatists varied the character of the music between every act, as may be seen in plays where the directions for music between the acts have survived[2].

[1] Mr Welch points out (*Six Lectures on the Recorder*, p. 131, note 2) that Henry VII and Henry VIII employed *still-minstrels*.

[2] Cf. *Gorboduc*, before Act I. violins, II. cornets, III. flutes, IV. hautboys, V. flutes and drums; or *Tancred and Gismunda*, before Act II. still-pipes, III. hautboys, IV. a consort (viols and lutes); or *Sophonisba*, after Act I. cornets and organ, II. recorders and organ, III. organ, viols, and voices, IV. treble viol and bass lute; or *Jocasta*, before Act I. viols, cithern, and bandurion, II. flutes, III. cornets, IV. trumpets, drums and fifes, and "a greate peale of ordinaunce was shot of," V. still-pipes.

CHAPTER IV

INCIDENTAL MUSIC

Overtures—Trumpet blasts—Songs—Entr'actes—Dances—Calling for tunes—Dancing after the play—Supernatural Music—Mr Pepys and the recorder—Melodrama.

ALTHOUGH music was introduced with the utmost freedom into the action of Elizabethan plays, there were certain conventional uses observed corresponding to the part a modern theatre orchestra fulfils in playing an overture, entr'actes, and accompanying songs, or in playing music to increase the emotional tension of a scene. Indeed our use of the orchestra in pure drama is a debt we owe to the men who made English drama. Our English custom of associating music with drama must have been handed down from the time of Shakespeare. It cannot be a loan from opera ; for since the days of Davenant and Purcell, opera in England has always been a forced and outlandish kind of drama, never fixed in popular support, but flourishing when the fashionable world lent its approval, and dying when it turned its fickle face another way.

In the age of Shakespeare, no overture was played before the curtain rose. There was no curtain to rise. The custom was to play three blasts on the trumpet or sackbut from the topmost story before the speaker of the prologue entered to speak his lines. It was no new thing to blow trumpets at the beginning of a meeting. It was common at tournaments and at fairs. The church had done the like on certain feast-days. In some places musicians were sent up the church-tower to play before the celebration of festival masses. The custom still lingers in a few old-world towns. In parts of Germany, a quartet of brass instruments plays chorales at Christmas before the service. The May-morning singing on the tower of Magdalen College at Oxford is a similar relic. A "cheerful noise of trumpets" was sounded before the overture in seventeenth century Venetian opera[1]. Wagner copied the custom in introducing fanfares of trumpets outside his theatre at Bayreuth before the performance.

There is no lack of evidence for this custom, as may be seen by the following allusions. Greene's *Alphonsus, King of Arragon* (1599) begins with the note "After you have sounded thrice, let Venus be let down from the top of the stage[2]." Ben Jonson was fond of introducing his characters on the stage in a humorous "induction," and in the course of the dialogue he indicated where the trumpet-blasts were to be sounded. Such inductions written for *Every Man out of his Humour* (1599) at *The Globe*, and for *Cynthia's Revels* (1601) at *Blackfriars*, prove that the custom of sounding thrice was followed at both public and private theatres. Dekker alludes to it in his *Guls Horn-Booke* (1609). "Present not yourselfe on the stage (especially at a new play) untill the quaking prologue hath (by rubbing) got culor into his cheekes, and is ready

---

[1] See *La Verità mascherata* (*Riemann-Festschrift*, Leipzig, 1909) cited in article "The Baroque Opera" by E. J. Dent in *The Musical Antiquary*, January, 1910.

[2] Venus would descend upon a hoist lowered from beneath the "heavens," *i.e.* a sounding-board which projected over the balcony.

to give the trumpets their cue that hee's upon point to enter" (Chap. VI).

Probably the custom lingered until the theatres were closed in 1642. There are references to it in the inductions to Heywood's *Four Prentices of London* (1615) and to *Lady Alimony* (ca. 1633). From the latter, and from Jonson's inductions, it is clear that the three fanfares were not played consecutively, but that an interval of a few minutes was made between each.

If there were songs in a play, and usually there were, the consort of viols and lutes in the music-room played the accompaniment. Sometimes, as in the case of Shakespeare's serenades, musicians came out on the platform to play the accompaniment. Sometimes the singer himself played a viol da gamba or lute, accompanied most likely by other musicians in the music-room; but directions for this are found almost entirely in plays performed at the private theatres, and the inference is that as these plays were performed by choir-boys, who presumably had some knowledge of music, such scenes were arranged to show off the little actors' attainments.

In the "act-time," or break between the acts of a play, musicians usually played. Sometimes there was pure music, sometimes a dance or a song. Sometimes no break was made between the acts, especially if the next act simply carried on the tale, and it was not wished to indicate a time-interval. Music between the acts dates from the beginnings of English drama. *Gammer Gurton's Needle* (1566) has references in the dialogue showing that music was played between Acts II and III. The custom crept into early attempts at tragedy in the shape of musical accompaniments played to dumb-shows. *Gorboduc, Jocasta, Tancred and Gismunda*, and *The Misfortunes of Arthur* all have directions for musical dumb-shows. From early comedy and tragedy, entr'acte music passed into regular use on the public and private stage. Very few plays contain directions for music between the acts, but the testimony of Prynne and of contemporary playgoers indicates that dance-music was customary between the acts.

Directions for music between the acts occur in *The Blind Beggar of Bednall Green* played at *The Rose* playhouse in 1600[1], also in Marston's *Sophonisba* (1606) played at *Blackfriars*. His *Parasitaster*, which was also done at *Blackfriars*, in the same year, has directions for a short dumb-show before Act V, "whilst the Act is a-playing." There are no stage-directions for music between the acts in *The Knight of the Burning Pestle* (ca. 1610), but the epilogues to each of the first three acts containing the comments of the Citizen and his Wife show that the musicians played, and after Acts I and III a boy enters and dances. Actual dances between the acts, as well as dance-music, appear to have been common. An early play, *The Two Italian Gentlemen*, by Anthony Munday, specifies the dances, namely, "a pleasant galliard," "a solemn dump," and "a pleasant allemaigne[2]." Greene's *James IV* (1598) has the direction "Enter a round, or some dance at pleasure" at the end of the fourth act. Sometimes songs were introduced between the acts. A chorus accompanied by organ and viols sang after Act III in *Sophonisba*, but references to songs between the acts are very rare.

There is evidence that patrons of the drama used to cry out between the acts for tunes they fancied. A delightful bit of satire in *The Knight of the Burning Pestle* arises out of this. At the end of Act II "the fidlers go again,"

[1] See article by W. J. Lawrence in *Shakespeare Jahrbuch* XLIV.
[2] Cited by J. P. Collier, *Annals*, Vol. III. p. 448.

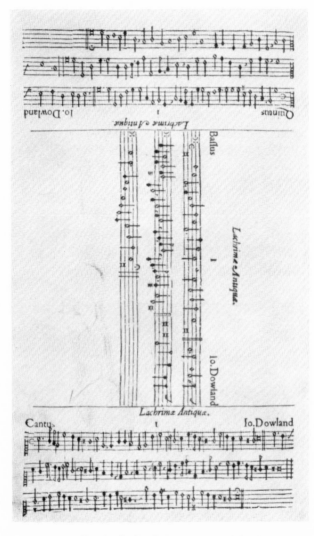

Dowland's *Lachrimae* arranged for four voices,

Plate VIII

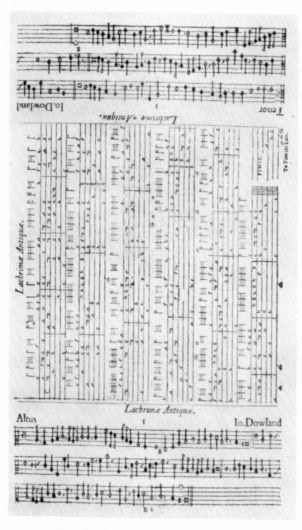

accompanied by viol da gamba and lute

and the Citizen calls "You musicians, play Baloo" (the name of a tune). "No, good George," entreats his wife, "let's ha' Lachrymae." "Why, this *is* it, cony," he replies. *Lachrimae* is a "pavane," that is to say a slow dance in common time, by the John Dowland referred to in *The Passionate Pilgrim* (Sonnet VIII). To us it seems a dreary, dirge-like tune, but it was tremendously popular amongst the Elizabethans[1]. It is to be found twice, adorned with all manner of contrapuntal divisions, in the *Fitzwilliam Virginal-Book*, also in Morley's *First Booke of Consort Lessons* (1599), and in Dowland's *Second Booke of Songs or Ayres* (1600).

Further evidence that the audience called for tunes is to be found in Sir Bulstrode Whitelock's *Memorials*. He composed a dance-tune called *Whitelock's Coranto*, which was often played at *Blackfriars* by the band "who were then esteemed the best of common musitians in London." The tune was very popular and was "often called for[2]." When music was played between the acts, it would consist of either "ayres," that is, songs arranged for stringed instruments, or of popular dance-tunes such as galliards, pavanes, jigs, dumps, almains, corantos, and the like. Every tune had its proper name just as the tunes have in a modern hymn-book—indeed the names which have clung to old psalm-tunes are simply a survival—and the audience shouted these names—"Baloo," "Lachrimae," and the like—when they wanted a change of tune[3].

---

[1] It is referred to in the following plays : Jonson's masque *Time Vindicated*; Massinger's *Maid of Honour* (Act I. Sc. 1); *Picture* (Act V. Sc. 3); and Middleton's *No Wit like a Woman's* (Act I. Sc. 1). *Lachrimae* has been recently reprinted in Breitkopf and Härtel's *Euterpe*, No. 7.

[2] Burney's *History of Music*, Vol. III. p. 376.

[3] There is an interesting scene in Thomas Heywood's *A Woman Killed with Kindness* (Act I. Sc. 2), where the servants of Master Frankford are

If dancing was fairly common between the acts, it was still commoner at the end of a play. There were, of course, the jigs and jests of pipe and tabor players like Tarleton and Kempe, but also at the end of some plays the actors finished with a dance. *Much Ado About Nothing* ends with Benedick's exhortation, "Strike up, pipers," and the direction "Dance." In *As You Like It*, the Duke's couplet, almost at the end of the play :

> "Play, music ! and you brides and bridegrooms all,
> With measure heap'd in joy, to the measures fall,"

indicates that a contra-dance was performed before the epilogue. Even after tragedies they danced. Thomas Platter, a visitor from Germany in 1599, tells in a letter to his friends in Basel how he went to a Bankside theatre in the afternoon and saw *Julius Caesar* acted by about fifteen players. At the end of the play four men danced, two being dressed as women[1].

Another use of music that must be recorded was to produce or to enhance a supernatural effect. When supernatural beings descended from "the heavens" in the hoist, it was usual for music to be played. For example, amongst the additions to *Doctor Faustus* in the quarto of 1616 there is a scene where a good and a bad angel come to visit Faustus before his awful end. The good angel ascends to heaven in the machine, and as the hoist descends, music is directed to play—probably to hide any noise made by the machinery. Pepys records another instance in his diary for 27th February, 1668. On that date he saw Massinger's

---

having "a crash" in the courtyard. They resolve to dance, and debate whether the tune shall be "Rogero," "John come kiss me now," "The Cushion Dance," "The Hunting of the Fox," or "The Hay." Finally, they call on the music to strike up "Sellenger's Round."

[1] *Anglia*, Vol. XXII. p. 458.

Virgin Martyr, a poorish play but finely acted. "But that which did please me beyond anything in the whole world, was the wind-musique when the angel comes down." It made him feel, he tells us, as he used to feel when he was in love with his wife, and he thereon resolved "to practise wind-musique" and to make his wife do the like[1]. This supernatural effect was obtained by the music of recorders, for on the 8th April we find Mr Pepys going to buy a recorder: "which I do intend to learn to play on, the sound of it being, of all sounds in the world, most pleasing to me."

If a supernatural "vision" occurred in a play, such as the visions in *Pericles, Cymbeline,* or *Henry VIII,* the stage-directions indicate solemn music. Also where Shakespeare introduces mythological figures he directs music, doubtless to increase the supernatural effect. "Soft music" is directed for the entrance of Iris and Ceres in *The Tempest* (Act IV. Sc. I). "Still music" ushers Hymen on the stage in *As You Like It* (Act V. Sc. 4). Music in the shape of songs is associated with minor supernatural beings. Shakespeare's fairies, whether real as in *A Midsummer Night's Dream,* or pretended as in *The Merry Wives,* sing songs. The witches in Middleton's *Witch,* and the river-god in Beaumont and Fletcher's *Faithful Shepherdess,* proclaim their supernatural character in their songs.

But the most interesting, and, to musicians, perhaps the most important experiment is the use of music to increase the pathos of a scene. The opening scene of *Twelfth Night* is perhaps not a case in point, because it may be objected that the music is introduced to delineate the Duke's character; but a clear instance is to be found in

---

[1] Cf. the beginning of Jonson's masque *The Golden Age Restored* (1615), "Loud music: Pallas in her chariot descending, to a softer music."

the scene in *The Merchant of Venice* where Bassanio
chooses his casket. There Portia calls for music which
continues whilst Bassanio soliloquises on the crisis before
him. Marlowe, whose fondness for the sensuous appeal of
music we have already seen, introduces music to enhance
the pathos of Zenocrate's death (2 *Tamburlaine*, Act II.
Sc. 4). Physicians are preparing bootless medicines, and
Tamburlaine and his sons surround the bed. Zenocrate
calls for music, and Tamburlaine bursts into a tempest
of sorrow and passion as she dies.

Another typical instance is to be found in Marston's
2 *Antonio and Mellida* (Act I. Sc. 2). As Pandulpho be-
wails the death of his son in a speech, which though stoical
in tone is charged with deep feeling, " music sounds softly "
as he begins, and it swells to " loud music " as his emotion
increases. Several examples are to be seen in Beaumont
and Fletcher, notably the one in *Thierry and Theodoret*
(Act III. Sc. 2). In this there is dramatic irony. Just
before he is murdered, Thierry calls for soft music to
" drown all sadness." Similarly in *The Revenger's Tragedy*
(Act III. Sc. 4), Vendice wreaks the death of his mistress
on the Duke. The Duke dies from the kiss of her poisoned
skull to the sounds of music from a banquet " within."

A blend of melodrama and supernatural music is used by
Shakespeare (assuming the scene which we shall quote from
Pericles to be his) in two of his plays. The idea underlying
both scenes is the power of music to restore the dead to
life. Readers of *The Winter's Tale* will remember how (in
Act V. Sc. 3) Hermione is presented as a statue to Leontes
by her friend Paulina, and how she is brought to life by
music :

> "*Paulina.*   Music, awake her; strike!
> 'Tis time; descend, be stone no more; approach!"

and Hermione descends from the pedestal into the arms of her penitent husband. In *Pericles* (Act III. Sc. 2) Thaisa is awakened from her trance in the house of Cerimon, at Ephesus, by music :

> "*Cerimon.*   The rough and woeful music that we have,
>   Cause it to sound, beseech you.
>   The music there! I pray you give her air.
>   Gentlemen, this queen will live."

According to modern notions, both scenes are weak ; and one wonders what the author's motive really was. Did the music betoken a miraculous event, or was it used simply to enhance the emotion of the scene ?

These instances, which are not exhaustive, show that this dramatic use of music occurs in plays done at both public and private theatres. It is not a feature that deserves praise. Drama should be stark enough to stand alone, without the help of musical stimulants. But the pathetic use of music is not merely another inartistic feature of the decadence of romantic drama. It is deep rooted. It goes beyond early plays like *The Merchant of Venice* and *Tamburlaine* back to the Mysteries. In the Chester cycle, in the scene in the Drapers' play, where terror strikes the hearts of Adam and Eve when they hear the reproving voice of God, the minstrels played solemn music. And it has endured to our own age. What is a melodrama but a play where we expect to hear bombast and sentimentality accompanied by fitting music ?

CHAPTER V

MUSICIANS, SINGERS, AND SONGS

Strolling fiddlers—Alluded to by Dekker, Gosson, and Northbrooke—
Knight's statement—The Golden Age of English Music—Va-
grancy Laws—Theatrical musicians—The musical "aristocracy"
—Actors as musicians.

THE men who provided this music in the theatres were
a despised and outlawed caste, recruited from the ranks of
strolling musicians. They were despised by the church,
hated by Puritans, and mocked at even by a writer of
plays like Dekker. Without visible means of support,
wandering from tavern to tavern and town to town, with
many ready to listen and few willing to pay, forced to tout
for a hearing and beg for a pittance, is it a marvel that they
were called thriftless and impudent? "As familiar as a
fiddler" seems to have been a proverbial saying[1], and
Dekker confirms it in his *Guls Horn-Booke* (1609) in the
chapter describing "How a Gallant should behave himself
in a Taverne" (Chap. VII). "If you desire not to be
haunted with Fidlers, who by the statute have as much
libertie as Roagues to travell into any place, having the
pasport of the house about them[2], bring then no women
along with you." It was this impudence and brazenness
that drew on their heads the wrath of beneficed clergymen.

[1] *Wild Goose Chase*, Act II. Sc. 2.

[2] This refers to an Act of 39 Elizabeth which allowed minstrels and players
to stroll if they obtained a nobleman's Patent under "hand and seal of arms."

"London is so full of unprofitable pipers and fidlers that a man can no sooner enter a tavern than two or three cast of them hang at his heels," says Stephen Gosson in his *Short Apologie* (1587). John Earle tells the same story about a stage-trumpeter. There is "no man so much puft up. His face is as brazen as his trumpet, and, which is worse, as a fidler's, from whom he differeth only in this, that his impudence is dearer[1]."

There is little sting in these charges. They are the petty malice of men, fortunate enough to sell their gifts for a secure position in the commonwealth, against others who were compelled by the age to peddle their art for a beggar's dole.

But a more serious charge is brought against them by John Northbrooke, who, although a Puritan, was a lover of music. He defended it because it moves our senses with its sweetness and yet delights the reason "by the artificiousness" of its harmony and form. This man must have known also something of the time and aptitude required for learning the art of music, and yet he says "of minstrells that goe and range abroarde, and thrust themselves into every mannes presence" that they were insufferable "bicause they are loyterers and ydle fellowes; ...and, to saye truth, they are but defacers of musicke[2]." Idle doubtless they were, in the sense that all musicians and actors are idle, having easy-going and perhaps frolicsome intervals between the times when they concentrate their minds upon their mystery and give a public exhibition of their art. But why not? An executive artist cannot work with the same concentration as a tradesman or a field-worker. For one reason his brain cannot stand the strain, and for

---

[1] *Micro-cosmography*, No. 38.

[2] *Treatise against Dicing* (ca. 1577).

another he cannot have a perpetual audience. As for the charge that they were only "defacers of musicke," let us set over against it Knight's statement that the best musicians of the Kingdom were to be found in London, "and equall to any in Europe for their skill...in singing or for playing upon any kinde of musicall instruments[1]."

It was an age of music. Catches were sung by gentles as well as by weavers and tinkers. Lute, cithern, or virginals were in every barber's shop for the diversion of customers. They had music for dinner, after supper, for joy and for mourning, in the church and in the play-house. Thomas Morley may be using the biased argument of a music-teacher when he tells us that a gentleman was counted but a boor if he could not play the lute, or sing a part in a madrigal[2]; but there is no getting over the craggy fact that over eighty collections of Madrigals, Ayres, and Songs were printed and published between 1587 and 1630, in addition to which vast collections of early music still remain in manuscript[3]. Such a public was not likely to listen to mere defacers of music.

There may have been a few Crowderos with their "squeaking engines" left to make "souse to chitterlings," but the harshness of the laws against vagrancy must have thinned their tale. Under the Act of 14 Eliz. c. 5 (1572) minstrels and players were to be dealt with as rogues and vagabonds unless they owned a licence signed by two magistrates. In 1597 it was granted to noblemen to employ companies of players, including musicians, under a patent (39 Eliz. c. 4). This was repealed by James I

---

[1] "The Third Universitie of England." Appendix to Stow's *Annals.* Quarto edn. 1615.

[2] *Introduction to Practicall Musicke* (1597).

[3] Henry Davey, *History of English Music*, pp. 171—4.

in 1603, and henceforth strolling players, musicians, and their fellows were liable to be seized as common vagrants[1]. The common way of evading the law was for the theatrical companies to purchase warrants of protection from the Revels Office. The King's Company paid £1 for such a licence to play at *Blackfriars* in 1627. A similar warrant for twenty persons "all imployed by the Kings Maties Servants" as "musitions" and attendants at *Blackfriars* was granted in 1624[2].

The wandering musicians who went from tavern to tavern in small bands were, as we have seen, unloved of the respectable. They were known as "waits" when they played wind-instruments, and a "noise" if they played stringed viols and lutes. Some of them, it may be, were descendants of the minstrels and ballad singers of a previous age. Others were the product of the new rage for music. To them, as to the strolling players of Interludes, the founding of a permanent stage in London must have come as a godsend. We imagine the best of them being absorbed, along with perhaps a few Italians or "Venetions," into the permanent staff of the theatres. The theatres would also provide engagements for additional waits in certain plays. As for the rest, the devil in the shape of the vagrancy laws would take the hindmost in the rush for upland counties where the acts were not put in force.

As a class, theatrical musicians were no better and no worse than other bohemians of the age. Doubtless some, as far as their means would allow, were as dissolute as Greene and Marlowe. Others, like the Henry Walker from whom Shakespeare bought his house at Blackfriars

---

[1] Collier, *Annals of the Stage*, Vol. I. p. 203, and note; also p. 360.
[2] Malone, *Prolegomena*, Vol. III. p. 112, notes 6 and 7.

in 1612[1], became good citizens and men of property. At least it was an economic advantage to exchange the tip of the tavern or brothel for a fixed salary in the theatres. And it must have been an artistic delight, to say the least, to forsake the bawdy songs of the streets[2] for the lyrics of the stage. There is a reference to the scanty earnings of strolling fiddlers in Greene's *Orlando Furioso* (1594):

> "*Orgalio.* I can tell thee where thou mayst earn two or three shillings this morning.
>
> *Fiddler.* Tush, thou wot cozen me, thou: but an thou canst tell me where I may earn a *groat*, I'll give thee sixpence for thy pains."

This implies that a groat was good pay for a morning's work.

And so they exchanged the ragged cloak of a wandering minstrel for the licence and badge of a player, and no doubt they played better music, and played it better than ever they did in their lives before. But their followers in the next generation were driven back to the old haunts of the trade by the closing of the theatres in 1642. From the tavern they had originally come, and back to the tavern they went. "Our music, that was held so delectable and precious that they scorned to come to a tavern under twenty shillings salary for two hours," says the author of *The Actors' Remonstrance* (1643), "now wander with their instruments under their cloaks (I mean such as have any) into all houses of good fellowship, saluting every room where is company with: 'Will you have any music, gentlemen[3]?'" And the end of the story as far as it interests our period is Cromwell's re-enactment of the law declaring to be "rogues,

---

[1] Chappell's *Popular Music of the Olden Time*, edn. 1859, p. 252.

[2] See Earle's *Micro-cosmography*, No. 63.

[3] Cited by Collier, *Annals*, Vol. III. p. 450.

vagabonds, and sturdy beggars" any fiddlers or minstrels taken whilst making music in "any inn, ale-house, or tavern,...or desiring, or intreating any to hear them play, or make music, in any of the places aforesaid[1]."

It must not be supposed that all the musicians of Shakespeare's age were in this plight. The best musicians, men such as Dr Bull, William Byrd, Orlando Gibbons, Thomas Morley, Richard Johnson, John Dowland, and their fellows, were in regular employment as church organists, gentlemen of the Chapel Royal, or lutanists or virginal players at court or in noblemen's houses. They were well educated for the most part, and highly esteemed for their musical talents. They mingled with their patrons with as much freedom as did poets. These were the men who composed music for the song-books, and arranged the popular dances and songs of the day for small orchestras or "consorts" to play. And these men composed music for the songs in the dramas. Many of the songs are still in existence in the song-books of Byrd, Dowland, and Morley, and in manuscript[2].

Probably this aristocracy of music considered itself far above the vulgar in rank and breeding, and never stooped to take an actual part in theatrical performances. Beyond the appearance of Henry Lawes as Attendant Spirit in the private performance of *Comus* in Ludlow Castle on Michaelmas night, 1634, no record exists of a composer taking part in a play; unless by a coincidence, the Dr

[1] Cited by Percy in his *Essay on the Ancient Minstrels in England*, Note EE 2.

[2] The existing songs from Shakespeare's plays have been republished by Sir Frederick Bridge—*Songs from Shakespeare*, published by Novello. Bridge has also published Henry Lawes' songs written for Milton's *Comus*, along with some typical dance-music, in *The Masque of Comus*, with an Introduction by W. Barclay Squire, published by Novello.

John Wilson, whose song, "Take, O take those lips away," appears in his *Cheerful Ayres or Ballads* (1659), happens to be the singing-boy Jacke Wilson whose name is found in the Folio of 1623 as the actor who took the part of Balthasar in *Much Ado About Nothing*.

But if there was a line of demarcation between theatrical musicians and the aristocrats of the tribe, there was none in the theatre between musicians and players—that is to say, between musicians and the players paid by the shareholders, like themselves—for the players who held shares in the theatre formed another aristocracy. Musicians took minor parts on the stage as walkers-on in armies, masques, serenades and the like[1]. And probably players who only acted small parts lent their help to the music. We learn from the induction to Jonson's *Every Man out of his Humour* that the prologue was delivered by a sackbut-player[2]. There are references in the plays to singing-boys playing their own accompaniments. The player Phillips, in his will (1605), left his bass viol to Gilburne, his late apprentice, and his cithern, pandore, and lute to Sands, who was then his apprentice[3], which implies that Phillips and his apprentices helped the "consort" at times with viol and lute. In Heywood's *A Woman Killed with Kindness*, the boy who took the part of Mistress Frankford played a solo upon his lute in the last act. And in Middleton's *Roaring Girl*, the boy who acted as Moll, the heroine, played the viol da gamba and accompanied, or perhaps helped the consort to accompany, his song (Act IV. Sc. 1).

---

[1] Cf. also this direction in Greene's *Alphonsus, King of Arragon* (Induction), "Enter Melpomene, Clio, Erato, with their sisters, playing all upon sundry instruments," &c. These were players upon viols and lutes as the context shows.

[2] "I mar'le whose wit it was to put a prologue in yond sackbut's mouth."

[3] Malone, *Prolegomena*, Vol. III. p. 472, 1821 edn.

So that several of the players' boys were musicians as well as players.

With that we leave them. As a class they were no better and no worse than the rest of their fellows who manned the wooden O's of Bankside and the suburbs. As musicians, they managed to satisfy audiences who knew what music was, and it is only reasonable to suppose that regular employment in the theatre would give them greater skill to play the complicated rhythms of their music than touting for a hearing round the taverns.

The number of musicians employed in any given theatre is another matter that cannot be definitely decided. Malone's tradition tells us there were eight or ten[1]. *Blackfriars* theatre employed twenty men in 1624 as musicians and attendants, of whom we may reckon a dozen at most to have been musicians. But how are we to reconcile this few with the numbers of music-makers indicated in the stage-directions of some plays? If we suppose all of them to have been employed at once, the number could not well be less than say two viols, viol da gamba, bass viol, two or three instruments of the lute type, three cornets, three hautboys, three recorders, sackbut, and organ—a total of eighteen musicians for a private theatre; or, omitting organ, cornets, and recorders, and substituting drums and trumpets, a like number for a public theatre[2]. We must assume either that some musicians played several instruments, or that for certain plays additional musicians were engaged. Or possibly both these courses were followed. We

[1] Malone, *Prolegomena*, Vol. III. p. 111, 1821 edn.

[2] The usual number of musicians in the Jonson-Ferrabosco-Giles-Inigo Jones masques at Whitehall seems to have been eight, viz. five lutes and three cornets. See *Neptune's Triumph*, but "a rare and full music of twelve lutes" is mentioned in *The Masque of Hymen*. Also there are directions for additional harps, and drums and fifes in other masques.

have seen that the actors Phillips and Sands played three types of lute—lute, cithern, and pandore. And considering how similar in fingering were all the wood-wind instruments—cornets, hautboys, and recorders—it may be that some of the waits played them all. Remembering that variety in orchestration and not mass of tone was their custom, we may assume that in the private theatres eight or ten musicians could have played all the music required.

Further light on the subject is thrown by a survey of Henslowe's instruments at *The Rose* on Bankside. Henslowe's inventory of the properties of the Lord Admiral's Company was made on 10th March, 1598[1]. He found it in possession of three trumpets, one drum, one treble viol, one bass viol, one pandore, one cithern, a chime of bells, a sackbut and three "timbrells." The last may have been the kettledrums used for "alarums" (Fr. *timbale*). In addition to these another sackbut was bought, as his diary shows, on 10th November, 1598, and on the 22nd December in the same year "a base viall and other enstrements" were added. Reading between the lines, 1598 seems to have been about the time when music became an indispensable ingredient of drama in England. There are further entries relating to the purchase of a drum and two trumpets on the 6th and 7th February, 1599, but as they were destined to be used by the company on a spring tour[2] they do not concern us.

Now what were these instruments for? Were they the actual instruments used by the theatre musicians, or were they merely properties? They fall naturally into two

---

[1] Supplement to *Henslowe's Diary*. Shakespeare Society, 1845.

[2] Cf. Parolle's slander of Dumain: "Faith, sir, has led the drum before the English tragedians" (*All's Well* &c. Act IV. Sc. 3). Also, trumpets are indicated to signal the approach of players in *Hamlet* and *The Taming of the Shrew*.

classes. Obviously the sackbuts, trumpets and drums were not properties. They were the actual instruments used for the three blasts before the prologue, and for martial flourishes and alarums. The treble viol, cithern, pandore, and bass viol may possibly have been used simply as properties to hang on the walls when the stage represented an interior, but it is much more likely that they were used by the musicians. It may be objected that these instruments were Henslowe's, and that musicians like to play on their own. Well, it is not impossible that Philip Henslowe had them in pawn; but the simplest solution is that the musicians in regular employment at *The Rose* theatre left their instruments there over night. The stringed instruments form a complete quartet, and were the "consort" used for accompanying songs, and sometimes for playing between acts. These dozen instruments represent the music required in the public theatres, played by about half a dozen professional musicians, and assisted by a few musical players and their boys when necessary. That being granted, the "not received custom of music" at *The Globe*, mentioned in the induction to the Marston-Webster *Malcontent*, did not mean that Burbadge's company forwent music (as, indeed, the play itself shows); but it meant that they were without the cornets, hautboys, recorders, and organ of *Blackfriars* where the *Malcontent* came from. And perhaps the induction was written to take the place of music performed at *Blackfriars* before the play.

To sum up. It is difficult from the slender evidence before us to decide how many musicians were employed at a given theatre. Plays varied much in their musical demands; but we must suppose that small bands of regular musicians, some of whom played more than one kind of stringed and wood-wind instrument, were sometimes augmented by additional musicians. For the private theatres we may take Malone's tale of eight or ten as correct. The public theatres employed a smaller number on their staff, and engaged hautboy and cornet players when necessary.

A theatre company usually included one or more singers in its troupe. Both men and boys sang songs on the stage. The reigns of Elizabeth and James I stretched over an age of song. Singing was a fashionable accomplishment, and of the making of songs and the music thereto there was no end. Hence the popularity of songs in the drama. Shakespeare knew his audience well, and it cannot be a coincidence that the two plays whose titles imply that he was giving it what it wanted contain the most songs. *As You Like It* and *Twelfth Night, or What You Will* contain no fewer than six songs each. Certain rôles were created simply for singing men. Merrythought[1] and Stremon[2] could only have been acted by singers, and so also Balthasar[3] and Amiens[4] are simply an excuse for introducing a song. Pandarus[5], too, must have been taken by a musician, for he accompanied his song "Love, love, nothing but love" on his lute. The extremity of song-introduction is to be seen in the part of Valerius in *The Rape of Lucrece* (1608), to whom Heywood gives seventeen songs. Parts like Feste and Autolycus must have been taken by singers. Real clowns like Slender, Sir Toby and Aguecheek, Stephano, and the Fool in *King Lear* merely babble snatches of ballads and catches.

---

[1] In Beaumont and Fletcher's *Knight of the Burning Pestle*.
[2] In Beaumont and Fletcher's *Mad Lover*.
[3] In Shakespeare's *Much Ado About Nothing*.
[4] In Shakespeare's *As You Like It*.
[5] In Shakespeare's *Troilus and Cressida*.

Many of the best songs were sung by boys. Amongst Shakespeare's songs, Ariel's songs in *The Tempest*, and the fairy songs in *A Midsummer Night's Dream*, also "Take, O take those lips away" and Desdemona's Willow song were certainly sung by boys; so were the duets "It was a lover and his lass" (sung by pages in *As You Like It*) and the Dirge in *Cymbeline*. We have no means of judging whether serenades were sung by boys or by men. Most likely they were sung by lutanists who played their own accompaniments.

The songs of Elizabethan times may be roughly divided into (1) songs for voices alone, (2) songs accompanied by instruments. The former fall into two classes, Madrigals and Canzonets; or Catches, Rounds and Three-men's (or Freemen's) songs. Madrigals and Canzonets were of Italian origin, and have been described as "a few jingling rhymes set to elaborate music." The poems consist of single verses full of glossy diction about "spightfull dainty nimphs," "tormenting Love," and the "sharp and bitter anguish" of languishing lovers. They were set to music for voices in counterpoint, and were in fact simply a framework on which elaborate part-writing was stretched. The words were quite subordinate to the music. Madrigals took the place which chamber music now fills, but as they never became popular on the stage they do not concern us here. As poems, they are dainty little sweetmeats, but they soon cloy. As music, they are full of grateful vocal part-writing, and show a strong sense of rhythm, "snap," and syncopation. Catches, on the other hand, were in use on the stage. They are to be found in Shakespeare's plays, and in Beaumont and Fletcher. Dekker introduced Three-men's songs in his *Shoemaker's Holiday*. They were popular songs requiring merely a loud and persevering voice. It required a musician to bear a part in a madrigal, but any fool could join in a catch. They were canons for four, or in the case of three-men's songs for three, voices. The well-known "Three blind mice" is a good example. On the stage, as in real life, they were used in the merry-makings of jovial but not over-cultured good fellows.

The songs with musical accompaniment fall again into two classes—Airs and Ballets, or Songs. Airs were part-songs like madrigals, but differed in that they were accompanied by a consort of instruments. The words are written in stanzas. The musical time is usually simple and slow, and the music not without contrapuntal devices, but the intention was to make every part sing the same syllable at the same time in strict diatonic harmony. For example, the old psalm-tunes are "airs." Ballets were similar harmonic part-songs set to a dance measure. Songs were, of course, melodies for a single voice set to a harmonic accompaniment played by instruments. They were stanzaic, and usually the melody was repeated for each verse. This is always the case with folk-songs such as "O Mistress mine," "The rain it raineth every day," Ophelia's song, and Desdemona's song. Some of the songs written and composed for drama follow this rule; for example, Thomas Morley's setting of Shakespeare's "It was a lover and his lass." But many consist of only one stanza, *e.g.* Ariel's songs "Where the bee sucks" and "Full fathom five," set by R. Johnson; and some, like the Forester's song in *As You Like It*, and "You spotted snakes" in *A Midsummer Night's Dream*, have a "burthen" or chorus at the end of the stanza, being in fact half song, half "air."

Songs and airs were closely allied. The accompaniment being harmonic, the melody part of an air could always be sung solo. Byrd wrote his *Psalms, sonets, and songs of*

Plate IX

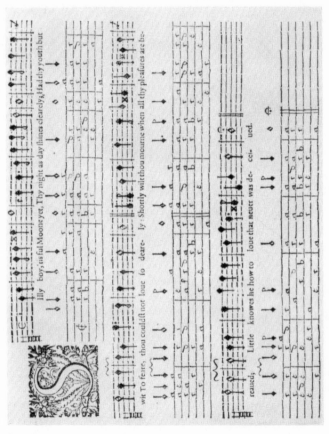

An Elizabethan Song with lute accompaniment (From Campion's *Third Booke of Ayres*)

sadness and pietie (1587) originally as songs, and then arranged them in parts. As he tells us in his preface, "beeing originally made for Instruments to expresse the harmony, and one voyce to pronounce the dittie, (they) are now framed in all parts for voyces to sing the same." John Dowland entitles his *First booke of songes or ayres* (1597) "of fowre partes with tableture for the lute: so made that all the partes together, or either of them severally may be song to the lute, orpherian, or viol de gambo"; and Robert Jones' *First booke of songes and ayres* (1600) bears the same legend.

It was songs and airs, with instrumental accompaniment, not unaccompanied madrigals, that were introduced into the drama. Tradition called for them. Had there not been songs in the drama since its beginnings in England? And popular taste demanded songs with a harmonic instrumental accompaniment rather than contrapuntal and italianate madrigals. Madrigals were always caviare to the general. This was fortunate for the art of poetry. What little sense the madrigal-poems had was almost destroyed by the crossing and interweaving of the part-writing. It was possible at times for each part to be singing different words, so fond were the Italians of vain repetitions. It was delight in counterpoint, not in poetry, that called them into being. But songs and airs were a tribute to the art of poesy. The melody aimed at bringing out the sense of the poem. The harmonic accompaniment built on a figured bass never obscured the words. If you were a composer you tried, says Thomas Morley (1597), "to dispose your musicke according to the nature of the words which you are therein to expresse." The words of the poem were all-important, and its melody simple and rhythmic, so that every word could be heard. Elizabethan songs were the product of a partnership between poet and musician. For their books of songs and airs, musicians sought the work of the best lyrists; and for dramatic songs, poets engaged the services of the best musicians. There was a direct incentive for poets to give their best songs to the drama. Hence the melodious lyrics of Dekker, Beaumont and Fletcher. Hence also Ben Jonson's studied strains, and the wild wood-notes of Shakespeare.

Solo songs in the published music books have a tablature for lutes to play from, and a bass for the viol da gamba. From this bass the skilled musicians of the period could extemporise an accompaniment on the virginals or organ, or fill in the harmony with viols. Airs or "consort songs" usually have an accompaniment scored for S. treble viol and lute, A. flute and cithern, T. pandore, B. viol da gamba[1].

The music played in theatres between acts consisted probably of selections of popular dances[2]. Airs arranged for the consort may have been played also, but dance-music was the natural thing because dances were often performed in the "act times." Also the tunes mentioned as having been called for—*Baloo, Lachrimae*, and *White-lock's Coranto*—are all dance strains. The music played for alarums, sennets, tuckets, flourishes and the like has perished entirely. Probably it was traditional amongst the theatre musicians—a part of their mystery; and this would account for its not being transcribed.

---

[1] See Plate VII. Dowland's *Lachrimae*, p. 68.

[2] Specimens may be seen in Sir Frederick Bridge's *Masque of Comus*, 1908, Novello.

CHAPTER VI

ELIZABETHAN MUSIC AND ITS SHARE IN
THE DRAMA

Elizabethan music —Its characteristics—Its popularity—Why and how
    introduced into drama— Dramatic value of music—Its emotional
    effect—Dramatic songs—Music and Romanticism.

IF the Elizabethan age was like " a nest of singing birds,"
and "the golden age of English music" as the critics tell
us, how is it that the best songs are not heard at our
concerts? The answer is that the songs as music, however
beautiful they may be as poems, have been left far behind
by later developments in harmony. The poems are still
read with lively enthusiasm, and the madrigals are a living
joy to some glee-societies; but the songs, the airs and the
dances are forgotten; save by a few cultured musical
antiquaries, who, after valuing Elizabethan music for its
historical importance, have learned to appreciate its beauties.

Owing to their diatonic nature, Elizabethan airs sound
like snatches of old psalm-tunes. They are all quaint,
many of them are pleasing and even powerful in their
emotional appeal, but, to ears accustomed only to modern
music, they are uttered in a dead language which sounds
often harsh and crude. The seventh note of the scale
is frequently left unsharpened, which conveys to modern
ears the effect of a change of key. This is owing to
the fact that their scales were hexachords. Another
peculiarity was that Elizabethan ears could tolerate a
"false relation." Leaps in the melody from a given
note to its imperfect octave (*e.g.* ♯F to ♮F) are sometimes

made, even in vocal music. Consecutive fifths are to be found; and in the same key, both major and minor thirds are often written in different common-chords on the same note. Yet in spite of its crudeness, their harmony fashioned some wonderful songs. Some of Dowland's, Morley's and Johnson's deserve to live for their sweetness, and as monuments of musical beauty worked in very simple harmonies. As an example of a simple melody depicting exactly the mood of the words, Wilson's setting of "Take, O take those lips away" is perfect. Their dance-music does not wear as well as their songs. Most of it consists simply of eight-bar strains strung together to make a short dance. It is pompous or jolly, or doleful according to its nature, but there are crudities of harmonic progression that jar.

Their virginal music is full of art. It was the age of counterpoint, and all the tricks of the art were employed in arranging popular melodies for two hands. A common custom was to take a well-known tune—a psalm-tune or a popular dance suited them equally well—and to write variations upon it, each in a different species of counterpoint. "Fancy" is the name they gave to another musical form in which the melody is given out fugato and elaborated with imitations and sequences. Another favourite form was the "prelude"—a study depending for its construction upon a series of chords elaborated with scales and arpeggios and ornamented with sequences. But virginal music was for the closet, not for the theatre.

To judge Elizabethan music aright, we must look at it in perspective. Modern music was then a new-born art. The shackles of the church modes were not completely cast off. Composers differed from all other artists in that they had to make their medium as well as their handiwork.

The painter or the writer had at least knowledge of colour or syntax at his fingers' ends, but the musicians actually had to make their art of harmony as they went along. All their gropings after pleasant progressions and new effects are to be seen in their music, and if Elizabethan music displeases modern ears it is because it represents a transition from Gregorian modes to major and minor scales, from counterpoint to the freedom and daring of harmony.

It is a curious fact and one worthy of note that there is no attempt in Elizabethan drama to satirise or even to poke mild fun at a musician. Spaniards and Dutchmen, Pedants and Poetasters, Beggars and Constables, Justices and Rogues, come in their turn under the lash, but not musicians. They were the priests of a new art, the interpreters of a divine harmony whose perfection was only to be heard by dwellers in the heavenly spheres. Shakespeare's Balthasar is affected, but so is Osric. The Shrew breaks her lute across Hortensio's head, but she also attacks Petruchio. Balthasar and Hortensio are not made a laughing-stock because of their profession like Shallow and Dogberry, or Don Armado and his fellow scrap-stealer Holofernes. It is their manhood that is impugned, not their musicianship.

And this gives us the key to the seventeenth century attitude to music. It was "sweet music," "the divine ravisher of sense," "divine sounds," and a whole host of epithets that link it with the uplifted trumpets and immortal harps of the seraphim. They idealised it. Earthly music was but the faint echo of the sphery chime

> "Still quiring to the young-eyed cherubims,"

or

> "That undisturbed song of pure content
> Aye sung before the sapphire-colour'd throne."

Thence came it that the dramatists satirised the starvelings who could not appreciate it, the Citizen who preferred the waits of Southwark to the skilled musicians of *Blackfriars*, and his wife who could not distinguish Lachrimae from Baloo ; or again, Bottom's "reasonable good ear in music" that demanded "the tongs and the bones."

Music was popular in the drama because it was popular everywhere. From puritan weavers singing the Hundredth Psalm in parts from Este's *Psalmody*, and the tavern-chanters with their catches, to the cultured singers of airs and madrigals, all ranks delighted in song. A gentleman's education was incomplete unless he could sing prick-song[1] or compose an extempore discant to a melody[2], or at least fiddle a bass on the viol. Musical instruments there were in plenty. If there were trumpets at court, and hautboys at feastings, there were lutes in the barbers' shops for all the world to strum upon. Almost every house of nobleman and burgher alike had its virginals. Pepys in his diary of the Great Fire of London (1666) observed that as the citizens fled the fire by water "hardly one lighter or boat in three, that had the goods of a house in, but there was a pair of virginals in it." This was written sixty years after our period, but it must have been true in part for Shakespeare's day.

Given this musical public, one can see why music became firmly associated with the stage. They wanted to hear the best songs. So quite naturally the theatres fell in with popular taste and provided songs for their patrons. Elizabethan dramatists wrote lyrics as free and as polished as the best lyrists of the age, for were they not poets? The playwright, that rule-of-thumb carpenter of French extraction, who builds you an introduction, a tangle, and

---

[1] That is, a printed part in an air or madrigal.
[2] Cf. Morley's *Introduction to Practicall Musicke* (1597).

Plate X

A "Broken Consort" (German, end of 16th Century)

a *dénouement* into a prose "drama" of three acts, was still in the future.

Shakespeare's audiences went to the theatre to hear music. They demanded it. They expected it. They were critical of it. If a play was displeasing to the gilded youth of the age, they not only mewed at the "passionate speeches" but they found fault with the music and whistled at the songs[1].

There were no "rules" for the introduction of songs, and little attempt at art in their introduction. There are sublime exceptions, of course. Ophelia's ballad and Desdemona's song are intensely dramatic. But at first sight it seems as if one song were as good as another, so long as it were good. Most of the songs in Beaumont and Fletcher are simply sops flung to popular taste. The serenades and singing-boys (such as the pages in *As You Like It*, or Balthasar in *Much Ado*) of Shakespeare are simply an excuse for introducing a song; so is the singing-boy in Jonson's *Silent Woman*. Yet a further inspection shows some sense of fitness. Folk-songs, or skilful imitations, and ballad snatches are often put in the mouths of comic characters. Fairies have their own characteristic songs, and so have witches. And the finest lyrics of the dramatists, those which best express their characteristic powers—short, melodious, spontaneous, polished songs, full of imagery and point—were set to music by contemporary composers and were usually sung by singing-boys. If catches were introduced, they were sung by representatives of the lower orders—apprentices, soldiers, beggars and the like.

Usually a play had at least one song. That was the musical *pièce de résistance*, but, as we have shown, there

[1] Dekker's *Guls Horn-Booke* (Ch. 6).

was often music between acts. Again music entered into the scene realistically. It came on with an army. The shrill cry of the trumpet and rattle of drums made six supers appear a mighty host. It came on with masquers or serenaders. Their stage-dances and songs were a copy of the music of real life.

Music was added also to increase the emotional tension of a scene. The tragic songs of Ophelia and Desdemona are the supreme examples. But they are very rare. Usually the effect of introducing music with an intent to increase the emotional force of the scene is not dramatic, but melodramatic. Bassanio choosing a casket to the sound of music, Zenocrate's death accompanied by a pathetic strain from the music-room, what are these but attempts to gild the pure gold of poetry with superfluous tinsel? More to be commended is the introduction of music to delineate character. The music in *Twelfth Night* tells us much concerning the character of Count Orsino. The music which Brutus hears on the night when Caesar's ghost appears to him is another feature which distinguishes the conspirator Brutus from Cassius the traitor. Jacques' song with its burden "ducdame," and Hamlet's scene with the recorders, both enable us to know them better.

But though music on the stage was realistic in that it was a copy of music in real life, in effect it was highly romantic. However rigid in form, however constrained in harmony it may be, music is always romantic. Its beauty of melody, its discords resolving on concords, its rhythm, its form, the characteristic tones of the different kinds of instruments, all make a wonderful emotional effect. It can excite or sadden our feelings more than the spoken word. Hence music was welcomed on the stage as a rival to poetry in beauty and emotional force.

Shakespeare and his fellows said in effect: "Music is an additional beauty, therefore let us include it in our drama." Their lyrics wedded to music moved men to mirth or sadness in a more poignant way than words alone could do. And this brings us face to face with two questions that challenge us and must be wrestled with before we pass on. Was their use of music an artistic success? Did Elizabethan drama gain, or lose, by the addition of songs?

Of music between the acts, whether dance measures or song-tunes, we shall say nothing. If actors must rest and properties must be changed, there can be no harm in beguiling the interval with music suitable to the play. Dancing between acts seems at first less defensible. We at once think of eighteenth century play-bills of *Hamlet, Prince of Denmark* in which Mr So and So "will dance a hornpipe between Acts three and four." But Shakespeare's age was not as unutterably tasteless as that. They had many characteristic dances—stately pavanes and almains, the gay jig and the lively brawl, and the tearful dump to express sorrow; and they used taste and discretion in introducing them. Dancing after a tragedy again is quite easy to defend. The Greeks had their satyric drama at the close of a trilogy. The neo-classicists allowed a farce. They who wish the theatre to be a moral force will naturally object to anything which blots out the sense of tragic purification. They object to any distraction after a tragedy. But to ordinary sane people who regard the theatre as an intellectual recreation, a dance at the end is simply as the fifth act of *The Merchant of Venice*, and is to be defended on that ground—namely, that it comes as a relief after the tenseness of tragic emotions.

What is to be said about their alarums, flourishes,

sennets and tuckets? The answer can only be that they are a blot upon drama. This is not the objection of a lover of classic simplicity and restraint. The most bigoted romanticist must admit that to drag drums and trumpets on the stage on every possible occasion was simply an appeal to the groundlings who were "capable of nothing but noise." It was to turn the theatre into a circus. Trumpet flourishes might have been dignified if they had been used rarely, and only for scenes of great splendour, but they were made too cheap. No one will be prepared to defend stage battles of five supers and a drum. The only thing that can be said in favour of "alarums" is that if such sorry spectacles had to be introduced in face of the audience, alarums helped the impression of warlike confusion and clash of arms. But this stage-direction was another concession to popular taste.

Incidental music was not always an artistic success. One cannot cavil at the custom of introducing supernatural beings with music. Employed here, music lifted the action out of the every-day world. Something is necessary to indicate that the marvellous is happening. Flames must burn blue, or we may miss the fact that our visitor is a spectre; and where the dramatists introduced mythological persons, music was a pleasant and an artistic convention. But when they used music to intensify the emotion of a scene in which men and women were taking part, the result is not often happy. Shakespeare's use of music to delineate Orsino's character in *Twelfth Night* is good, but Marlowe's death of Zenocrate with slow music is sentimental and trashy.

To turn next to songs, the most important use of music on the stage. We owe surely a great debt to music for calling into being a number of lyrics by the elder dramatists that have enriched English literature for all time. If their drama had been bound in the shackles of neo-classical "rules" there would have been no music and we should have had no songs. We can forgive their banal alarums and "soundings," which we have not to endure, for the delight of their lyrics. But if we can imagine ourselves dramatic critics in the Elizabethan age forced to visit every new play—and who would not give ten years of his life if such a revisitation could be?—what could we say about their songs? We should be forced to admit that but few of them assist the unity of action, and that there is simply no excuse for the introduction of many of them. For example, Beaumont and Fletcher's *Rule a Wife and have a Wife* has a song introduced into Act III. Sc. I, without the least dramatic significance. Altea says "Let me have a song." The stage-direction reads "Song by the boy," but otherwise he does not appear in the play, and there is actually no direction for his exit.

Songs introduced like this, without any reference to the action of a play, but merely in deference to popular liking, cannot be defended even by the most romantic romanticists. And there are many such, especially in Beaumont and Fletcher's plays. Serenades and masques are nearly as undramatic, but at least the song is introduced in a suitable setting. Some of them also, like Cloten's serenade, or the masque of Madmen in Webster's *Duchess of Malfi*, do contribute to the unity of action. These have dramatic meaning, but it must be confessed that, as often as not, serenades and masques were merely an excuse for introducing the song.

The only legitimate reasons for introducing a song, to one who wishes a play to be a drama and not a pageant, are to create an atmosphere, as for instance the songs in Arden, in *As You Like It*; or to delineate character, *e.g.*

Feste, Ariel, Autolycus, Amiens ; or to create an emotional effect in tragedy, *e.g.* Ophelia's and Desdemona's songs, or to take an example from Beaumont and Fletcher, Aspatia's fine song in *The Maid's Tragedy*. The few songs that occur in romantic tragedies are almost without exception skilfully introduced and tremendous in their emotional effect. It was in comedy that they gave way to popular prejudice, and damaged their dramas as works of artistic unity by the meaningless introduction of songs.

In conclusion, let us sum up the value of music to the drama of Shakespeare's age. Undoubtedly the wedding of music to drama is a loss if the ideal drama is to be a poem with a skilful plot which rushes to an inevitable end. If the neo-classic ideal be right, music has no place in drama. It enters into unfair competition with poetry for the verdict of our emotions. It calls a halt in the middle of the dramatic coil, it tends to diffuseness, and often breaks the unity of action. But the drama of Shakespeare and his fellows admitted no neo-classical restraints. It demanded complete freedom and strove continually for new levers to move emotion.

Music was emotional in its effect, therefore it was welcomed. It brought colour and variety into the drama. The very orchestration, the combinations of instruments indicated in stage-directions, show love of beautiful and bizarre effects. It gave also realism to the action because it was always a copy of the way music was employed in common life. Granted our English romantic drama, music fitted naturally and inevitably into it, and can we forget its influence on lyric poetry? For its influence on the songs of the dramatists alone it has won the right to receive greater recognition than has hitherto been granted to its share in the production of an Elizabethan play.

CHAPTER VII

SOME LITERARY ALLUSIONS TO MUSIC IN ELIZABETHAN PLAYS

Musical imagery—Jonson's musical realism—Beaumont and Fletcher's use of music—Shakespeare's realism—His praise of music—His technical knowledge—Music in character delineation.

THERE are many allusions to instruments of music in our elder poets, and an interesting list might be compiled showing the uses of the various sorts. But not until the Elizabethan age did music provide materials for poetic imagery. The medieval poets in mentioning music piled instrument on instrument. Thus in *The Squyr of Lowe Degre*—

> "There was myrth and melody
> With harpe, getron, and sautry,
> With rote, ribible and clokarde,
> With pypes, organs and bumbarde,...
> With fydle, recorde and dowcemere,
> With trumpette and with claryon clere."

And so in *Piers Plowman*, the poet is not content with saying he cannot play music, he must emphasise the fact by cataloguing the accomplishments of a wandering minstrel:

> "Ich can not tabre, ne trompe, ne telle faire gestes,
> Ne fithelyn at festes, ne harpen,
> Japen, ne jagelyn, ne gentillische pipe,
> Nother sailen, ne sautrien, ne singe with the giterne."

We can easily imagine how one of our early poets would have interpreted the following thought from Marlowe's *Tamburlaine* (Act II. Sc. 4):

> "The cherubins and holy seraphins
> That sing and play before the king of kings
> Use all their voices and their instruments
> To entertain divine Zenocrate."

Stringed instruments provided many Elizabethans with a simile. In *David and Bethsabe*, Peele compares Absalon's hair with the "golden wires of David's ivory lute"—which instantly brings to mind Shakespeare's simile of Love in *Love's Labour's Lost*:

> "as sweet and musical
> As bright Apollo's lute, strung with his hair."

It would be idle to make a list. Their allusions are sometimes commonplace—

> "Sound forth Bellona's silver-tuned strings"
> (*Mucedorus*),

or sometimes striking—

> "I'll bear me in some strain of melancholy,
> And string myself with heavy-sounding wire,
> Like such an instrument that speaks merry things sadly"
> (*Revenger's Tragedy*),

but rarely beautiful. Shakespeare's superiority as a dramatic poet is plainly shown in his musical similes. He sings, his fellows simply jingle. How charged with the music of poetry is this passage from 1 *Henry IV*!—

> "thy tongue
> Makes Welsh as sweet as ditties highly penn'd,
> Sung by a fair queen in a summer's bower,
> With ravishing division, to her lute."

A new admiration for the power of music over men's emotions comes into literature in Shakespeare's age—the power which Dryden depicted in his *Ode for St Cecilia's Day*, "the spirit of that sweet sound" which Shelley panted for. Shakespeare felt it constantly, as his allusions and stage-directions indicate; and Marston, whose plays contain many interesting experiments in the stage use of music, puts this admiration into the mouth of Syphax in *Sophonisba*:

> "Hark! Hark! now softer melody strikes mute
> Disquiet nature. O thou power of sound,
> How thou dost melt me!"

It may be interesting and profitable to compare the attitude of three great Elizabethan dramatists towards music by contrasting their allusions in the text of their plays.

Ben Jonson is fond of mentioning music and musicians in a jocular way. Morose, for instance, is the victim of musical practical jokers in Jonson's *Silent Woman*. Clerimont schemes to bring music, Morose's pet abomination, to his wedding. No need to invite them, he thinks, "the smell of the venison going through the street will invite one noise[1] of fidlers or other"—a skit at the native "German bands" of the period. At the mock-wedding, Cutbeard excuses the gruff voice of the parson who is to unite Morose and Epicœne in wedlock, by telling Morose that he has been "sitting up late and singing catches with clothworkers"—an allusion to the Calvinist exiles from France and Flanders who earned their living by weaving.

---

[1] Noise meant harmony, as in the Authorised Version of Psalm c., "Make a joyful noise unto the Lord," or Milton's *At a Solemn Music*, "That we...may rightly answer that melodious noise"; but it was also a cant word for small bands of musicians who played from tavern to tavern. In *2 Henry IV*, Act IV. Sc. 4, the first drawer bids his mate "See if thou canst find out Sneak's noise."

After the wedding, Morose curses Cutbeard for marrying him to a shrew. " I have married his cittern," he wails, "that's common to all men." This is an allusion to the citherns kept in barbers' shops for customers to wile away the time until their turn came[1]. Barbers also practised as tooth-pullers, so Truewit suggests ironically that since Morose is set up as a barber by marrying a cithern, he should draw his own teeth and " add them to the lute-string "; or in other words string them in a chain on a lute-string to hang up as a trade-sign. In the same play also, Clerimont brings a bearward with his trumpeters to the wedding festivities of Morose. The bearward bids the trumpeters play whilst the guests drink : " Sound, Tritons of the Thames ! " After the fourth blast, Morose, who is stung to frenzy by the slightest noise, rushes out of the house with a long sword, and drives the " music " away.

Another musical joke occurs in his *Poetaster* (Act II), where Jonson ridicules the vanity of singers. Hermogenes, when asked to sing, refuses. His friends however continue to press him to sing, and, after protesting that he cannot sing, he reluctantly consents. After he has sung once, the next difficulty is to stop him. He is so pleased with himself that he desires nothing better than to go on with his singing; but they refuse to listen to more, and excuse themselves by saying they will hear his wonderful voice later.

Beaumont and Fletcher's use of stage-music is peculiar. They have no musical imagery in their verses worth quoting, and they do not delight in reproducing the musical

---

[1] In *Every Man in his Humour*, Wellbred compares a "gull" to "a barber's virginals, for every man may play upon him." See also Lyly's *Midas*, Act III. Sc. 2.

life of their times save in one respect—the regular association of music with wantonness. " Wine and wenches you shall have once again, and fiddlers," says, not Dr Martin Luther, but the Friar in *The Bloody Brother* (Act IV. Sc. 2). Musicians are "toys to prick up wenches withal[1]." It would be too sordid to go through all the passages dealing with music in this sense[2], but it is evident that music was sometimes used basely in the Elizabethan age.

Stephen Gosson accuses broken-down musicians of keeping immoral houses : " If any part of musicke have suffered shipwrecke and arrived by fortune at their finger endes, with shewe of gentility they take up faire houses, receive lusty lasses at a price for boordes, and pipe from morning till evening for wood and coale. If their houses bee searched, some instrument of musicke is laide in sighte to dazell the eyes of every officer ; all that are lodged in the house (are said to) come thither as pupilles to be well schoolde[3]." Rowland's *Doctor Merrie-Man* (1609) deals also with a " profest courtezan," who remarks :

> " I have my daintie Musicke playes
> When I would take my rest[4]."

But let us get out of the mire. Beaumont and Fletcher are often wilfully and intentionally sordid, but we forget it in the beauty of their verse. " He was so great a man that I had forgotten he had such a defect " must always be posterity's attitude to a great artist.

We turn with a sense of relief to Shakespeare. Like

---

[1] *Thierry and Theodoret*, Act I. Sc. I.

[2] See *Valentinian* (Act II. Sc. 6) ; *Elder Brother* (Act III. Sc. 5); *Knight of the Burning Pestle* (Act III. Sc. 4) ; *A King and No King* (Act V. Sc. 2).

[3] *School of Abuse*, Shakespeare Society, 1841, p. 26.

[4] Cited in Stubbes' *Anatomy of Abuses*, New Shakspere Society, Vol. I. p. 280.

Jonson, he alludes playfully to the musical life of the day. Aguecheek " plays o' the viol de gamboys." Falstaff lost his voice in his youth " hallelujahing and singing of anthems " (2 *Henry IV*, Act I. Sc. 2), hence his desire to sing like a Calvinist *émigré*, " I would I were a weaver, I could sing psalms or anything " (1 *Henry IV*, Act II. Sc. 4). Like Beaumont and Fletcher also, Shakespeare knew the seamy side of musical life. " See if thou canst find out Sneak's noise ; Mistress Tearsheet would fain hear some music," says the Drawer in 2 *Henry IV* (Act IV. Sc. 4). Cleopatra calls for music, the " moody food of us that trade in love " (*Antony and Cleopatra*, Act II. Sc. 5) ; and there is surely a reference to this use of music in the Friar's warning to Mariana in *Measure for Measure* (Act IV. Sc. 1):

> " music oft hath such a charm
> To make bad good, and good provoke to harm."

But Shakespeare's outlook on music was pure. He valued it highly. For him, music was a synonym for sweetness. A brook makes " sweet music with the enamell'd stones." Love is " as sweet and musical as bright Apollo's lute." Ophelia sucked " the honey " of Hamlet's " music vows." And Shakespeare believed that sweet music is a refining and civilising force " ordained to refresh the mind of man after his studies or his usual pain[1]." There is—

> " nought so stockish, hard, and full of rage,
> But music for the time doth change his nature.
> The man that hath no music in himself,
> Nor is not mov'd with concord of sweet sounds,
> Is fit for treasons, stratagems, and spoils.
> The motions of his spirit are dull as night,
> And his affections dark as Erebus."
>
> (*Merchant of Venice*, Act V.)

[1] *Taming of the Shrew* (Act III. Sc. 1).

Hence Polonius' desire that Laertes should "ply his music[1]." Shakespeare believed with Plato in the Music of the Spheres. There are many references thereto in his plays[2]; and the most magnificent—the hackneyed quotation from *The Merchant of Venice* (Act V)—surpasses the common conception of the eight spheres humming in solemn diapason.

> "Look how the floor of heaven
> Is thick inlaid with patines of bright gold:
> There's not the smallest orb which thou beholdest
> But in his motion like an angel sings,
> Still quiring to the young-eyed cherubins.
> Such harmony is in immortal souls;
> But, whilst this muddy vesture of decay
> Doth grossly close us in, we cannot hear it."

For Lorenzo, safe with Jessica in the garden of Belmont under the kind light of the southern stars, every star in the firmament joins in a chorus to be heard only by immortal souls.

There are several instances in the plays where music was introduced as a medicine. Shakespeare believed the words he put into Prospero's mouth, namely that a "solemn air" is "the best comforter to an unsettled fancy." In *2 Henry IV* (Act IV. Sc. 2, Folio I), where the king swoons in the Jerusalem chamber, Warwick calls for "music in the other room" to soothe the dying king. Three other examples occur in doubtful plays. In *Pericles* (Act III. Sc. 2) Thaisa is awakened from her trance by music, and in the last act Marina sings to ease the troubled mind of Pericles.

---

[1] *Hamlet* (Act II. Sc. 1).
[2] Cf. *Antony and Cleopatra* (Act V. Sc. 2), *Pericles* (Act V. Sc. 1), *Twelfth Night* (Act III. Sc. 1), *As You Like It* (Act II. Sc. 7). A good account of the Music of the Spheres is to be found in an article by Mr E. W. Naylor entitled "Music and Shakespeare" in the *Musical Antiquary*, April, 1910.

Again in *Henry VIII* (Act III. Sc. I), Queen Katherine
calls for one of her maidens to disperse her troubles with
a song. The boy who took the rôle of the maiden sang
the song "Orpheus with his lute" to an accompaniment on
his own lute :

> "In sweet music is such art
> Killing care and grief of heart."

There are rather similar references to the charm of
music in *The Tempest* (Act V. Sc. I), where Prospero
releases Alonso and his court from the magic spell, and
chases away with music "the ignorant fumes that mantle
their clearer reason." And in *The Winter's Tale*, the statue
of Hermione is brought to life by the power of music
(Act V. Sc. 3).

This idealisation of sweet music was accompanied by
much technical knowledge. Shakespeare knew that viols
and lutes were "fretted[1]." He knew that lutes were hard
to keep in tune[2]. He knew that easing the pegs of a viol
or lute upset the relations of the strings and introduced
discord[3]. He knew the fingering of a recorder[4]. He had
some knowledge of the gamut[5], and in *King Lear* (Act I.
Sc. 2) gives a most violent discord, the notes Fa, Sol, La,
Mi, for Edmund to utter as a musical pun on the theme
"discord." Perhaps the old rime was familiar to him :

> "Mi contra Fa
> Diabolus est in musica."

But in Sonnet 128, Shakespeare makes a curious slip. He
calls the keys of a virginal "jacks," whereas the jacks were

---

[1] "Though you can fret me, yet you cannot play upon me" (*Hamlet*,
Act III. Sc. 2).

[2] *Taming of the Shrew* (Act III. Sc. I).

[3] "O! you are well tuned now, but I'll set down the pegs that make this
music" (*Othello*, Act II. Sc. I).

[4] *Hamlet* (Act III. Sc. 2).

[5] *Taming of the Shrew* (Act III. Sc. I).

quite distinct from the keys. Lyly recognised this in *Midas* (Act III. Sc. 2), where he speaks of "the Jackes above" and "the keyes beneath." Jacks were wooden slides, that held the spikes of quill which struck the strings of the virginals. In the mechanism they correspond to the hammers of a pianoforte.

That Shakespeare had a remarkable faculty for observation is well seen in his numerous allusions to music in the shape of puns and quibbles on musical terms, but they are of interest now chiefly to the musical antiquary. Most of them are explained in Mr E. W. Naylor's interesting book called *Shakespeare and Music.*

In his knowledge of music to delineate character, Shakespeare is wonderfully true. It is impossible to draw hard and fast rules about lovers of music. Sometimes most unlikely persons are devotees, but, as a rule, men of action are not musical. Musical natures need leisure, and like poets, shrink from the stern and saddening reality of life into the refuge of an ideal world of beauty. Hence Shakespeare makes his soldiers scorn music. Hotspur would rather hear his brach howl than hear Lady Mortimer sing[1]. Benedick marvels that "sheep's-guts should hale souls out of men's bodies[2]." Mercutio scorns to be classed as a minstrel[3], and it will be remembered that Mrs Quickly says Prince Hal broke Falstaff's head for likening the King "to a singing man of Windsor[4]." But Shakespeare imagined also that men who really disliked music were treacherous.

> "The man that hath no music in himself,
> Nor is not mov'd with concord of sweet sounds,
> Is fit for treasons, stratagems, and spoils."

[1] *1 Henry IV* (Act III. Sc. 2).
[2] *Much Ado* (Act II. Sc. 3).
[3] *Romeo and Juliet* (Act III. Sc. 1).
[4] *2 Henry IV* (Act II. Sc. 1).

Hence Caesar mistrusts Cassius because "he hears no music[1]." Shakespeare deliberately pictures Brutus, the other conspirator, as fond of music. Was it because he loved him?

Turning to Shakespeare's heroines we find that gentle natures are usually described as being fond of music. Lady Mortimer and Lady Percy sing[2]. Bianca, as befits such a dutiful girl, is musical.

> "She taketh most delight
> In music, instruments, and poetry."
> (*Taming of the Shrew*, Act I. Sc. I.)

Juliet and Jessica are sympathetic to music. Hero, Silvia, and Imogen can be wooed with a serenade, whereas masculine types like Beatrice and Julia have no liking for music. Desdemona "sings, plays and dances well[3]," and like Ophelia, sings her swan-song in an intensely tragic scene.

Only one complete music-lover is drawn by Shakespeare. That is Count Orsino in *Twelfth Night*. His musical taste is the product of his sentimental nature. He recalls a strain with such sweet harmonies that its "dying fall" cloys with a single repetition (Act I. Sc. I). He delights in funereal songs (Act II. Sc. 4). In his feminine softness and sentimentalism, Shakespeare condemns the folly of utter devotion to music. Shakespeare valued music as one of the civilising influences of life, but he observed that the musician's humour is "fantastical." His ideal was a many-sided man, not a precious stone with a single facet.

It would seem that Shakespeare was not an instrumentalist (unless perhaps he had some slight skill on the

---

[1] *Julius Caesar* (Act I. Sc. 2).   [2] 1 *Henry IV* (Act III. Sc. 2).
[3] *Othello* (Act III. Sc. 3).

recorder), but his acquaintance with the gamut, his knowledge of the names of notes, rests, bars, and such technical terms as division, discant, pricksong, frets, &c., argue
that he had more than a poet's acquaintance with the art of
song.   So that it is probable that he bore a part in many
a madrigal, and his triumph as a song-writer may be due in
part to his feeling for musical rhythm, and his knowledge
of singing.   His musical and dramatic gifts went hand in
hand.   It is worth noting that all his songs are appropriate
to the dramatic action.   Even songs like " It was a lover "
in *As You Like It*, and Feste's *Come away, death*, though
intended to delight the groundlings, are in sympathy with
principal characters in the play.

At the same time, Shakespeare felt that the theatre
existed for drama and not for music.   Where, in the person
of Hamlet, he speaks as a critic of acting, he condemns the
groundlings because they are " for the most part...capable
of nothing but inexplicable dumb-shows and noise."   Dumb-
shows were pantomime accompanied by music.   Noise is
a common Elizabethan synonym for music, though in this
passage it may stand for rant.   It would not be a wild
conclusion to believe that Shakespeare, in this passage, was
attacking the popular craving for music in drama.   At the
time when it was written his company was feeling the
severe competition of the musical boys of Blackfriars.

Shakespeare is the supreme type of a truly cultured
poet, free from pedantry, but blessed with such power of
observation that all the arts of life are an open book to
him, and with such poetic gifts that the things seen become materials for building up characters and plots.   The
golden age of English drama was "the golden age of
English music," and in Shakespeare that music receives
its highest tribute of appreciation.

BIBLIOGRAPHY

Books concerning the Elizabethan Stage

Victor Albright. The Shakesperian Stage.
William Archer. Article in *Shakespeare Jahrbuch*, Vol. XLIV.
W. W. Greg. Henslowe's Diary. 1904.
Harold Child. The Elizabethan Theatre (*Cambridge History of English Literature*, Vol. VI. ch. x).
J. Payne Collier. Annals of the Stage. 3rd edn. 1831.
Malone. Prolegomena to Shakespeare. Ed. Boswell. 1821.

Books concerning Music and the Stage

E. W. Naylor. Shakespeare and Music.
E. W. Naylor. Article "Music and Shakespeare" in *The Musical Antiquary*, April 1910.
L. C. Elson. Shakespeare in Music.
J. W. Lawrence. Article in *Shakespeare Jahrbuch*, Vol. XLIV.
Anon. Article "Early Elizabethan Stage Music" in *The Musical Antiquary*, October 1909.

Books concerning Elizabethan Music

Thos. Morley. A Plaine and Easie Introduction &c. (1597).
Bacon's Sylva Sylvarum (1627).
Burney's History of Music.
Hawkins' History of Music.
Chappell's Popular Music of the Olden Time.
Chappell's Popular Music of the Olden Time. 2nd edn. Ed. H. E. Wooldridge.
E. F. Rimbault. Preface to Purcell's *Bonduca*.
E. F. Rimbault. Preface to *Parthenia*.
E. F. Rimbault. Musical Illustrations of Percy's *Reliques*.
Oxford History of Music, Vol. II.

Henry Davey. History of English Music.
E. Walker. History of Music in England.
Wilhelm Bolle. Die Gedrückten Englischen Liederbücher bis 1600.
Francis W. Galpin. Old English Instruments of Music.
Christopher Welch. Six Lectures on the Recorder.

REPRINTS OF ELIZABETHAN MUSIC

Musical Antiquarian Society's Publications, 1841, 1842, including:
    Wilbye. *First set of Madrigals.*
    Weelkes. *First set of Madrigals.*
    Bateson. *First set of Madrigals.*
    Bennett. *Madrigals for Four Voices.*
    Dowland. *First set of Songs.* 1597.
    Gibbons. *Madrigals and Motets for Five Voices.* 1612.
    Gibbons. *Fantasies in Three Parts.*
    Morley. *First set of Ballets.*
    Parthenia. Edited by E. F. Rimbault.
And the following more recent publications:
Fitzwilliam Virginal Book. Ed. by Maitland and Squire. Pub.
    Breitkopf. 1899.
Songs from Shakespeare. Ed. by Sir J. F. Bridge. Pub. Novello.
The Masque of Comus. Ed. by Sir J. F. Bridge. Pub. Novello. 1908.
Euterpe. Ed. by C. Kennedy Scott. Pub. Breitkopf.
The Triumph of Oriana. Pub. Novello.

APPENDIX

NOTES ON THE ILLUSTRATIONS

1. FRONTISPIECE. A photograph, by Mr Emery Walker, of part of a picture in the National Portrait Gallery representing scenes from the life of Sir Henry Unton. The plate shows an Elizabethan consort playing music at his wedding-feast. A procession of masquers is filing past the musicians, who are seated around a table with their music before them. The instruments played by the consort, beginning at the left, are viol, flute, lute, cithern, viol da gamba, and probably pandore. The violist rests his instrument against the chest, and not, as do modern fiddlers, under the chin. The gambist is depicted in an impossible attitude, holding his bow by the point. Here, evidently, the painter was at fault. At the top of the stair, on the right, stands a drummer; and on the left, a quartet of singers are shown. The period is the last decade of the sixteenth century.

2. PLATE I, p. 22 (from the *Encyclopaedia Britannica*, 11th Edition), is borrowed from an article in *Shakespeare Jahrbuch*, Vol. XLIV, entitled "The Fortune Theatre," by Mr William Archer. The plate represents a reconstruction of the first *Fortune* Theatre, in Golding Lane, by Mr W. H. Godfrey, from the original specification furnished to one Peter Streete, a builder, on January 8th, 1600, by Philip Henslowe and Edward Alleyne. The indenture is quoted by J. P. Collier in his *Annals of the Stage* (3rd edn. 1831), Vol. III. p. 304. The theatre was eighty feet square outside, and fifty-five feet square within. It was built of timber and plaster in the Elizabethan style, on a foundation of piles and concrete. The galleries were twelve and a half feet from front to rear, and were built in three tiers, the lowest being twelve feet high, the middle eleven, and the topmost nine feet high; and were floored and benched with wood. "Rooms" or boxes were provided, and like the staircases, they were plastered and ceiled. The stage was forty-three feet wide, leaving a space of six feet on each side between the platform (which jutted out twenty-seven and a half feet into the yard) and the lowest gallery. In front of the platform was a fence of oak pales. The pillars supporting the "heavens" were square pilasters surmounted by carved

satyrs. The tiring-house was fitted with glazed windows. The "heavens," staircases, and galleries were thatched with tiles, and the first was provided with a leaden gutter to carry away the rain. The old *Fortune* Theatre was destroyed by fire in December, 1621.

3. PLATE II, p. 24. A photograph (supplied by Messrs W. H. Smith & Son) of the so-called *Globe* Theatre "built upon the lines of" the above specification at Earl's Court in 1912.

4. PLATE III, p. 26. This is a half-size drawing of a plan of the Masquing House at Whitehall by Inigo Jones (Lansdowne MSS. 1171, Fo. 10) in the British Museum. No scale is given. The artist's name is signed on Fo. 9. The stage with its back-cloth and "wings" appears to be very like a modern stage, with the exception that steps lead down from the middle of the front to an orchestra or arena in the midst of the auditorium, where doubtless the dancing was performed. Between this dancing-floor and the stage, on the left side, the "musick house" is indicated. Its floor appears to have risen tier above tier like the auditorium, an arrangement quite suitable for musicians who are playing from music placed upon music-stands, witness the modern arrangement of an orchestra at any hall where orchestral concerts are given. There is nothing in the plan to indicate what the box at the right side of the stage was used for. The box in the centre of the auditorium was probably the royal box.

A writer in *The Quarterly Review*, Vol. CII. p. 423, describes the old banqueting-hall at Whitehall, built in 1606, as having been surrounded by two tiers of boxes, the lower supported by Tuscan, the upper by Ionic pillars. Opposite the stage was the box for the king and royal family.

Probably the seating arrangements for masques varied. Other plans in Lansdowne MSS. 1171 show more boxes than does Fo. 10.

5. PLATE IV, p. 44. A photograph of drums and trumpets in the Donaldson Museum at the Royal College of Music, London. They are described by the curator as (1) *Trumpet* (German), eighteenth century. (2) *Trumpet* (English), dating from the reign of George III. (3) *Drum* (Italian), seventeenth century. (4) *Drum* (French), eighteenth century. A drum in the Victoria and Albert Museum, South Kensington, identical with the latter, is there described as a "Tabourin de Provence." Although this plate does not represent Elizabethan instruments (which indeed are exceedingly rare), the instruments shown are probably very similar to the drums and trumpets used on the Elizabethan stage. For permission to photograph these instruments

and those shown in Plates V and VI, the author is indebted to the kindness of Sir George Donaldson.

6. PLATE V, p. 54. A photograph of wind instruments in the Donaldson Museum. (1) *Cornet* of ivory (described by the curator as French, sixteenth century). (2) No. 162, *Musette* (French), eighteenth century. A survival of the hautboy type. The only difference between musette and hautboy or shawm is that the latter had a broader bell· (3) No. 87, *Flute à bec* (French), sixteenth century. The instrument was called "Recorder" in England (ca. 1400—1700) and was afterwards known as the English Flute, or "Flageolet"—not to be confused with the French flageolet, which had four holes in front and two behind. (4) *Horn* of copper (described by the curator as German, seventeenth century).

7. PLATE VI, p. 58. A photograph of stringed instruments in the Donaldson Museum. They are labelled : (1) No. 91, *Viol* (French), seventeenth century. (2) No. 7, *Cither* (German), eighteenth century. This is the same instrument as the Elizabethan Cittern or Cithern. The carved head is worthy of note. (3) *Lute* (no date). (4) No. 3, *Viol da Gamba* (English) by Barak Norman (1692). (5) No. 9, *Archlute* (Italian), sixteenth century.

8. PLATE VII, p. 60. Specimen of a lute tablature from *A New Booke of Tablature* (1596) in the British Museum. Mr W. Barclay Squire gave much kindly help in pointing out this, and the subjects of the two following plates, as suitable for reproduction.

9. PLATE VIII, p. 68. A double page from Dowland's *Lachrimae* (Brit. Mus. K 2 i 16), representing the tune arranged as an "Air." The song-book was placed in the middle of a rectangular table. At each side sat two singers, and the lutanist and the player on the viol da gamba occupied seats at each end of the table. The lutanist played from the tablature, the gambist from the bass part.

10. PLATE IX, p. 86. One of Thomas Campion's songs with a tablature for a lute accompaniment. This photograph illustrates such solo songs as were accompanied on the stage by the singer himself, *e.g.* "Love, Love, nothing but Love" in *Troilus and Cressida*.

11. PLATE X, p. 92. A photograph of a manuscript illustrating a "broken consort" (Brit. Mus. Egerton MSS. 1554, Fo. 2), described as "German, end of sixteenth century." The instruments played by members of the consort, beginning at the left, are sackbut, cornet, viol, lute, viol da gamba or bass, and organ. Two singers are depicted on the left of the picture, and the organ blower is to be seen on the right.

INDEX